H F PRINTS

Sixty years of reindeer on the Cairngorms

Emily Singleton

To Mum, and all my family,

*who's optimism when faced by life's challenges,
never falters.*

ACKNOWLEDGEMENTS

I am so grateful to such a large number of people, both friends and family, who have provided invaluable help to me throughout the making of this book. I hope I have not failed to mention any of those to whom I am particularly grateful. Without you all, this book would not have been possible.

Firstly, to everyone who has given me their time to share their own personal accounts, photos and stories of both Mikel Utsi and Dr Lindgren. You have all helped me to come closer to 'knowing' them both a little more. From speaking to you all, it is clear they both left a very large impression on many people's lives. It has been a joy to learn about them and I have therefore found it particularly difficult to write about them, but you have all helped tremendously, so a big thank you to James Lang Brown, Jonathan Potts, John Lindgren, Wendy Bishop, Enid Clarke and Alan and Tilly Smith. I would also like to thank all the staff at Reindeer House, Fiona, Heather, Hen, Andi, Gill, Jack and Anna, who, despite being extremely busy with the reindeer and the Centre, and being exhausted much of the time, have still helped to locate photographs and other important reindeer records for me. You have all been so encouraging and helpful. I would also like to thank Catriona, for her sharp eye in editing and willingness to help, regardless of the time or day. Lastly I would like to share my enormous appreciation of Tilly and Alex for helping me write this book. You have been so supportive throughout and have been a huge encouragement to me. Tilly, you have kept a guiding eye over the whole process and been incredibly helpful by rifling through the seemingly never ending mountain of archives. Yours and Alan's life with reindeer is an inspiration to so many people. Alex, having unlimited access to your wonderful photographs has been so helpful, and I hope I have done them justice. Thank you to all for keeping me sane through the process of this book (for the most part). On that note, I must also thank 'Tip the dog' for providing a very important distraction from the computer!

If they were here, I would thank Mikel Utsi and Dr Lindgren, for successfully re-introducing reindeer to Scotland. They are such wonderful animals to be amongst. I hope that eventually, everyone in Britain has a chance to meet the reindeer here, as I'm sure they would all agree- they really are something special. To all those 'reindeer adopters' over the many years, thank you for your ever-continuing support of the herd. Your devotion to the reindeer is gratefully felt by everyone at the Reindeer Centre.

Throughout this book are newspaper cuttings from various papers, photographs from various sources and writings from Company records. Despite much of it being carefully recorded, some of the original material had no information regarding copyright. I have tried to credit every photographer or writer for their work where possible; I apologise for any ommissing.

CONTENTS

INTRODUCTION

Reindeer have lived in Scotland since 1952 in the Cairngorm National Park where the herd are permitted to graze, upon an area totalling 10,000 acres. Within this vast and mountainous landscape grow an abundance of small shrubs, sedges, herbs, mushrooms, and lichens, all of which are of utmost necessity to the well-being of reindeer.

Now sixty years on, the herd is thriving. The reindeer are frequently seen and checked by a small number of herders. The herd is managed throughout the year and numbers are controlled through breeding. The Reindeer Council, was established in 1949 and subsequently, the Reindeer Company was set up as a trading company. The Company now derives its income primarily from the public by way of tourism. Over the years, the reindeer have become an important part of the community. The Reindeer Centre, based in Glenmore, was amongst the first buildings to exist in Glenmore and pre-dates both the arrival of the Scottish Sports Centre at Glenmore Lodge and the Cairngorm Ski Centre.

With over sixty years of hoofprints on the Cairngorms we celebrate Queen Elizabeth's Diamond Jubilee and also the 'reign of the reindeer' who were born here. This book celebrates The Cairngorm Herd, the people who have helped to make the project a success, and the Cairngorm Mountains, which we have come to call our home.

The Cairngorm Reindeer Centre would like to thank everyone who has helped to make the return of reindeer, who now roam in Scotland, a success.

Since their re-introduction, the Cairngorm Reindeer have all been individually identifiable and have been extensively documented; births, ruts and deaths have been recorded and a number of scientific research projects have been conducted. Studies were made of the composition of the reindeer milk, the haematological values of the blood, the micro organisms found within the reindeer rumen and ground breaking work was achieved on the artificial insemination of reindeer. More recent studies have explored the effects and spread of tick-borne diseases and the correlation of weather patterns and the sex ratio of calves.

The original imports from Sweden are now 11 generations on and many reindeer have been born here. The majority of the herd have descended from just three highly successful breeding females: Vilda, Assa and Tilla. These three were selected in Sweden by Mikel Utsi and came across with him during his early consignments. Vilda arrived in the 3rd consignment from Sweden in 1954. She boasts the largest family tree in our herd at present and many of her descendents became highly succesful breeding females themselves, such as Cherry, Tjakko and Russia. Over the span of generations, both homebred and imported bulls have been bred from in order to address the close genetic groups within the herd.

Many of the landscapes in the Cairngorms have remained unchanged for thousands of years. Now new trees have taken root on the lower slopes of the reindeer pastures and skiing has become a major attraction on Cairngorm Mountain. Alongside these new additions live the reindeer herd. Reindeer, unlike their red deer cousins, do not harm the ground. They are not harmful to ground nesting birds and do not destroy young trees as do red deer, thus making them an ideal neighbour for the other residents of the Cairngorms.

The indigenous Sami of Northern Scandinavia have changed their lifestyle from their traditional roots of living nomadically and using the reindeer as beasts of burden. For those families who continue to live by reindeer, herding with helicopters, bikes and ski-doos and living in permanent homes is now standard practice. As there is less direct interaction between the Sami people and their reindeer, the latter are are thought to be reverting to their wilder nature.

The methods of present day herders in Scotland are as traditional now as when they were once taught by Mikel Utsi. The 'herding' here remains a slow procedure; it takes time to gather and move the reindeer as all the work is achieved on foot. With the length of time spent amongst the herd, the herders have come to know the individuals within it. Just like people, each reindeer has its own unique features and character traits and it is the individuals of both herders and reindeer alike, and the subsequent relationships built between them, that make the reindeer herd of the Cairngorm Mountains a treasured sight for all who stumble upon them.

Mikel Nils Person Utsi was born on 17th May 1908 in Karesuando, the most northerly village in Sweden. He was the second of eight sons of a well-known Sami family.

Like other Sami families in the early part of the 19th century their livelihood revolved around the reindeer. Every spring the Utsi family would migrate with their herd of reindeer up to the mountains and across to the Norwegian coast. The reindeer were their main source of food, their skins were used for clothing and the large, castrated males were their beasts of burden, pulling the sledges which held all their possessions.

When Mikel Utsi was 15 years old, border politics between Norway and Sweden meant that the Swedish Sami of Karesuando were no longer allowed to move with their herds across the Norwegian border. The Utsi family along with many other Samis were relocated by the Swedish government. The migration route of their reindeer was forced to change.

The family was moved further south, to summer pastures in the Swedish mountains where the family established a new summer village, named Vaisaluotka. From here they had to train their reindeer to migrate south east, down the Luleå valley, to winter in the forests around Porjus, Jokkmokk and Murjek. Like refugees they had no choice but to move and start a new life.

As the second oldest son Mikel was expected to find his own way in life and his entrepreneurial spirit took him away from reindeer herding to running a chain of restaurants in the capital of Norrbotten, Luleå. He served three periods in the Swedish army and during the second world war played a pivotal role when, as a Swedish special constable, he and a colleague rescued from death many Norwegian refugees escaping the Nazis across the uninhabited border between north Norway and Sweden. For his bravery Mikel Utsi was awarded the Freedom Medal by King Haakon of Norway after the war.

Like other indigenous people, the Sami people with their unique culture and lifestyle have been the focus of many anthropological studies and in the 1930's and '40's Mikel Utsi was a great friend to visiting anthropologists who chose to work among the Sami. He spent many hours teaching them the basic elements of Sami etiquette, helping them to avoid an unintentional gaff often committed through ignorance of the system of manners and values of the Sami way of life. It was during this time that Mr Utsi met his future wife, the anthropologist, Dr Ethel Lindgren.

Right: Mikel Utsi in the family boat with his younger brothers, Paulus and Olle.

Mihkkels Biera, Per, Mikkel, John, Anders, Lars, Nicolaus, Paulus och Margareta, som kallades mor Dillá

Mikel Utsi amongst his family. He is standing third in line, behind his brother Per, and his father Mihkkel Biera. Photographed in the winter of 1919, North Sweden

MIKEL UTSI

Paulus, Olle, Mikkel bak
Foto: T. Dahllöf

13

Ethel John Lindgren was born on 1st January, 1905 in Evanston, Illinois USA, the only child of a wealthy Swedish-American banking family. As a young woman she travelled extensively with her mother and stepfather on his trips to the Far East. At fifteen, she visited Japan and China and at sixteen she made a Grand Cultural Tour of Western Europe. At seventeen, on another visit to China, she included a trip north to Kalgan, where she was impressed by the vast open landscape.

At the age of nineteen she was awarded a college scholarship to attend Newnham College, Cambridge to read oriental languages and moral science. Three years later, in 1924, she had completed her degree with first class honours.

In the same year she studied in China and then Mongolia. She made expeditions to Northern Manchuria, including ethnographic and social psychological explorations of its native communities, especially the Tungus peoples.

Between the years 1927 and 1932, she married Oscar Mamen, a Norwegian with experience of these regions, who accompanied her on expeditions and acted as photographer. The couple had one son, John Lindgren.

After this period, on return to England, she produced her doctoral thesis and what became her most recognised work, " Notes on the Reindeer Tungus of Manchuria", a study of Tungus society which included an interpretation of a Shaman's activities and function in the community.

Between 1934 and 1939 Dr. Lindgren made various trips to Swedish Lapland, conducting ethnographic studies. It was here that Dr. Lindgren, the anthropologist, met Mikel Utsi, the Sami.

Dr Lindgren led an academic career, lecturing in anthropology at Cambridge University and working alongside anthropological and psychological organizations. She taught methods of social research, anthropological field work, primitive religion, nomadism and the history of ethnographical theory.

During the Second World War she was a liaison officer at the Royal Institute of International Affairs at Chatham House, and after the war she returned to her work at Cambridge University. She was a council member of various Royal societies, including the Royal Geographical Society, Royal Anthropological Society and the Royal Central Asian Society. She was multi-lingual, and could speak fluent French, German, Swedish, Russian and Chinese. She had some knowledge of Dutch, Norwegian, Mongol and Tungus, being the first to rcord the language of the latter in the first written dictionary of the Tungus people.

In 1947, Dr Lindgren married her second husband, Mikel Utsi and retired from her academic career.

With her husband, Mikel Utsi, she devoted the latter half of her life to the project to re-introduce reindeer to Scotland.

Right: "Checking the calves"
Dr Lindgren sits on the ground next to the käta, bult by Mikel Utsi at the top of the Cairngorm enclosure. She is wearing her hobnail boots, for walking in the hills.

THE REINDEER COUNCIL
OF THE UNITED KINGDOM

1949-1950

Chairman : Sir Frederick Whyte, K.C.S.I.
Honorary Secretary : Dr Ethel John Lindgren, M.A.
Honorary Treasurer : Comdr. D.M Carmichael,R.N.V.R.
Technical advisor : Mikel Utsi.
Assistant Secretary : Mrs J.K.Smith

Members
William Brotherston, B. L
Geoffrey Bushnell, M. A. PhD
Louis C.G.Clarke, M. A.
Lt.-Col. N. A. C. Croft, D. S. O.
Lt.-Comdr. Douglas Dixon, D. S. C, R. N. (Retd.)
William B. Fagg, M. A.
Sir Graham Greene, K. C. B.
Miss Agnes Hicks, O. B. E.
Miss Isobel W Hutchison, L. L. D.
Hillar Kallas
Miss Helen G. Liddell, B. A.
F.A.G Medd
Ewan Ormiston
T.T.Patterson, M. A. PhD.
Lt.-Comdr. Quintin Riley, R. N. V. R.
Lt.-Col. Sir Michael Peto, Bt.
T.E. Utley, M. A.

"The Reindeer Exhibition" 8th March 1951

Mikel Utsi offers a plate of reindeer meat to members of the Council at the home of
Mr & Mrs Kallas, London..
L-R: Sir Arthur Tansley, Mikel Utsi, Sir Frederick Whyte, Miss Jemima Kallas, Mr
Wilson Harris.

Photo: 'The Sport and General Press Agency'

Extract from the Annual report 1949-1950

"On the 2nd of June 1949 a number of arctic experts, travellers, Scots interested in Highland development, and others met in London to inaugurate 'The Reindeer Council of the United Kingdom', and resolved that the object of the Council was "to encourage experiments in reindeer-breeding in suitable areas of Scotland and / or overseas, and to engage in any appropriate activity ancillary thereto.""

On a visit to the Highlands of Scotland, Mikel Utsi had discovered that much of the vegetation which grew there was similar to that of his homeland, where reindeer thrived. Ground, rock and tree lichens were in abundance in the Highlands, and they were of little use to other animals. After selecting a site for his proposed reindeer breeding experiment, he and his wife Dr Lindgren established The Reindeer Council of the UK. This was the first step towards the re-introduction of the reindeer, which had been absent from British shores for over 1,000 years. With written proof that reindeer had once roamed the North of Scotland back in the twelfth century, along with the welcomed idea of breeding the reindeer to provide an alternative meat source to post-war Britain, Dr Lindgren and Mr Utsi moved forward with their plans to re-introduce reindeer to Scotland by approaching the relevant authorities for approval. The Ministry of Agriculture gave them the permission they needed to begin their imaginative experiment, to breed a herd of reindeer in the Highlands of Scotland.

Mikel Utsi noticed an abundance of reindeer lichens growing in the north of Scotland that were not grazed by any other animal.

Right: An extract taken from the written report of 'Reindeer in Scotland', Mikel Utsi

"Looking across Rothiemurchus Forest to the Cairngorms from the railway bridge at Aviemore, on a cold morning in April 1947, I was instantly reminded of reindeer pastures. Travel in the Highlands showed that many species of ground, rock and tree lichens which are elsewhere the chief reindeer food were plentiful and of little use to other animals. Red deer and domesticated animals graze on plants and fodder that reindeer seldom eat. The Orkneyinga saga tells that about 800 years ago red deer and reindeer were hunted together, in Caithness, by the the Jarls of Orkney."

STAG PARTY

*The Reindeer Council of the United Kingdom
is proceeding with the experiment of importing
reindeer into Scotland.*

O LORDS *of misty moor and Ben!*
O monarchs of the mountain glen!
Crowned with your proudly branching span
Survey your kingdom while you can.

Where Affrie's corried glen divides,
In Atholl's furthest forest rides,
Amid the firs that fringe Loch Shin
Will feed the herds that fed the Finn.

Their splayed and hairy hooves will pound
Your ancient Highland stamping ground
And stalkers (snug in hats with flaps)
Will hunt the quarry of the Lapps.

Will later Landseers' art portray
Proud Scandinavian stags at bay,
And (taxidermic'ly prepared)
Will foreign heads delight the laird?

Will other antlers grace the walls
As hatstands in suburban halls-
Sad pointers to the fact that you
Have yeilded to the caribou?

Shall reindeer, blue of flesh and blood,
Reign where the ruling red deer stood,
Or will one more invasion fail
And wiser councils yet prevail?

Punch magazine.
Author unknown
August 1951

Across a rocky terrain
Dappled with heather still green.
Then over a brook by a fairy bridge,
Like those of which children dream.
On to a steep mountain side
That seems never to have tempted mankind,
As the purple bruised clouds are soothed by the sun
it reveals such a wondrous find.

There on the windswept landscape
The gentle reindeer stray.
Their sensitive antlers and soft wise brown eyes
Bring a magical touch to the day.
Be gentle to these creatures,
From a world of which we are part,
They will reward you with a moment of joy
that will warm and soothe your heart.

Written by Sara Dee, after visiting the herd,
June 2002.

21

REINDEER RESERVE

ROTHIEMURCHUS FOREST, INVERNESS-SHIRE

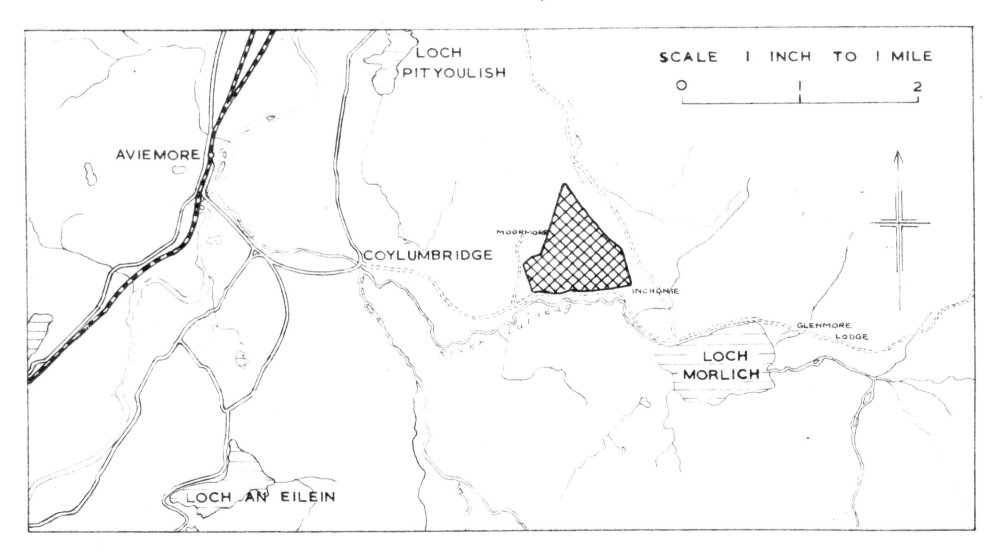

SCALE 1 INCH TO 1 MILE

0   1   2

LOCH PITYOULISH

AVIEMORE

COYLUMBRIDGE

MOORMORE

INCHONIE

GLENMORE LODGE

LOCH MORLICH

River Luineag

LOCH AN EILEIN

 PROPOSED REINDEER RESERVE — 310 ACRES —

MOORMORE RESERVE

The original site on Rothiemurchus Estate

Laird Offers a Forest Home for 14 of M'Neil's Swedish Reindeer

A home has been found for those Swedish reindeer Secretary of State Hector McNeil wants to bring to Scotland. It is on Rothiemurchus, near Aviemore.

It consists of 300 acres of forest land yielding all-the-year-round pasturage for 14 of the beasts- 11 fewer than first contemplated. The man behind the offer is Colonel E.P Grant, laird of Rothiemurchus and expert on deer, who has agreed to set aside the land for a three-year trial period. Much negotiation has still to be done, however, before Mr McNeil can give the O.K to Sweden.

'The Bulletin and Scots Pictorial'
August 4, 1951

Area of Reindeer Pasture

(Based on Sht. 43
O.S. 1-Inch)

Lt Col J.P. Grant, Younger of Rothiemurchus,
discussing future Reserve with Mr. M.N.P.
Utsi, outside Moormore Cottage. Col Grant's
Landrover to right.   No. 16

25

After much discussion on the appropriate site on which to attempt the reindeer experiment, Col John Grant of Rothiemurchus Estate agreed to let an area of unused pasture situated in the Rothiemurchus forest. The lease included the cottage of Moormore, a small and dilapidated structure. Work was done on the building to restore it to working order and it was ready by the time of the arrival of the first consignment of reindeer.

The land comprised 300 acres on the lower slopes of the Cairngorms. From the beginning Mr Utsi had voiced his doubts to The Reindeer Council members on the suitability of this low ground for the summer time but it was a foothold for the reindeer and close by to the higher ground further south. Once the letting agreement for Moormore had been signed the preparations began to construct a fence surrounding the proposed grazing site on Rothiemurchus Estate. It was nearly two miles long and conformed to detailed specifications. In spite of a heavy snow-fall, work began soon after Christmas of 1952.

Mr Utsi was assisted by two undergraduate volunteers, Mr James Lang Brown of Trinity College, Oxford and Mr George Webb of King's College, Cambridge. The wire for the fencing was "lent" by Messrs. Smith, Fletcher & Company of Edinburgh, and was transported to Rothiemurchus by the kindness of Mr Ormiston. Mr Utsi completed the fence with local help on his return from Sweden in April of that year. The interest and co-operation of many residents in the area had, throughout, been a great encouragement. The fence was finally 'closed' before the arrival of the first consignment of reindeer with the help of local volunteers and workers.

Moormore Cottage from the north, with the higher
Cairngorm pasturage behind.
March 1958
Photo: Edwin C Wakeling

Moormore, 1952

"

We went up by train to Aviemore and took a taxi to Coylumbridge, where we met Mikel at a tiny bungalow B&B, kept by a delightful couple who had fallen in love with Mikel. They were endlessly helpful and hospitable. We were off the next morning with a borrowed handcart and a bicycle to ferry our belongings, supplies and fencing tools up the long snow-covered track to Moormore Cottage - a deserted croft - lent to us by the estate. We young ones were cold but keen. Mikel knew how to survive in much tougher conditions than these. He had brought dried reindeer venison, a side of bacon and half a roe deer in Aviemore, along with oatmeal and vegetables. We didn't starve. We slept in the upper room where it was marginally warmer than the stone floor downstairs, in sleeping bags on reindeer skins. Mikel kept a Primus going all night keeping a brick nearly red hot. The work was hard - indeed really impossible.

We were not professional fencers and had no adequate fencing tools, but we kept at it, bouyed up by Mikel's optimism. By the end of a fortnight we had done much of it - not very tight or straight!

"

Above: Written by James Lang Brown

Far Left: Mikel pulls the 'borrowed cart' filled with equipment and belongings up the snow covered track to Moomore. January 1952.

Left: George Webb, fencing in the freezing and snowy conditions. January 1952.

RETURN OF THE REINDEER

The first consignments and their arrival by ship

New Clan Arrives

But Cannot Set Foot On Scottish Soil

By Sunday Dispatch Reporter

SCOTLAND'S first herd of eight reindeer, headed by five-year-old bull "MacRudolph", landed at Clydebank, Glasgow, yesterday-but were not allowed to put a foot on Scottish soil.

Restrictions against foot-and-mouth disease demanded that the deer should not touch the ground, and when the Swedish ship Sarek docked at the end of her 700-mile voyage the animals were taken ashore in crates, in which they had travelled on the boat-deck.

They will be released from their cramped quarters and allowed to step forth on land only when thay are delivered today to the quarantine section of the Edinburgh Zoo, where thay will stay for a month.

Extract from the 'Sunday Dispatch'
13th April 1952

The Cairngorm herd comprising 14 reindeer,
all looking to the Cairngorms
Winter of 1953
Photo: Aberdeen Journals

The first consignment of reindeer was taken from Mr Utsi's own mountain herd and consisted of 2 bulls, 5 cows, and a draught ox. For the duration of the journey, the reindeer were contained in crates on the Swedish ship, the S. S. 'Sarek', upon which the reindeer and crew had to endure a rather rough, four day crossing. The reindeer, in their boxes stowed behind the bridge, soon learned how to keep their footing and arrived safe and well on the 12th of April 1952.

At the Glasgow docks, the reindeer were lowered down from the ship in their crates by crane, and were kept for 28 days in a special quarantine block in the park of The Royal Zoological Society of Scotland at Corstorphine, Edinburgh before being transported by lorry to the prepared site at Moormore. On the 27th October that same year 10 reindeer of the forest variety arrived in Glasgow on the S.S Kalix.

The third consignment was not until 29th April 1954 which brought in 8 more reindeer. The fourth consignment consisted of just 2 Swedish bulls travelling free of charge on the S.S Erica Fritzen which arrived in Rothesay Dock on the 29th April 1955.

Many of these original imports bred successfully and have formed a strong foundation for the Cairngorm herd. More imports in subsequent years have helped to expand the gene pools further. On average the reindeer would spend 40 days between Sweden and the Cairngorms. With better transport and importation laws, recent journeys for consignments of reindeer have taken as little as five days.

Left and above: Upon arrival to Glasgow, the reindeer were lifted by a crane, from the Swedish ship S.S Sarek, in their wooden crates, and were met by both the public and the press.
13th April 1952

SILVERMOUNT *(Airgiod Meall)*

Extending the range and moving to higher pasture

Mikel Utsi and Kenneth MacLennan, the herder, sitting by the shelter on top of Silver Mount (Airgiod-meall), 2,118 ft above sea level.
This remains the highest point of the 1,000 acre enclosure.
26th July 1954
Photo: E. J. Lindgren

Moormore was let to the Reindeer Company from 1952 until 1954 as the agreement was held only for two years. During this time there were three consignments of reindeer. These reindeer formed the nucleus of today's herd. From 1953 the Forestry Commission allowed the herd to graze on a 70 acre plantation adjacent to Moormore, enabling the Company to demonstrate that there was no noticeable damage to conifers by reindeer.

Despite his gratitude to Col Grant and the Forestry Commission for making his initial plans a possibility, Mr Utsi always had his eyes firmly on the higher ground of the Cairngorms, as he had suffered losses in the herd due to insect harassment. He looked to gain permission to move and expand his experiment to breed reindeer in Scotland on the higher ground.

The Forestry Commission believed in the credibilty of the project and by 1954 allowed Mr Utsi to move his growing herd onto Airgiod-meall (Silver-Mount) on the northern slopes of the Cairngorms, which rises 2,118 ft above sea level.

The Reindeer Company were granted permission to extend their grazing rights further into the Cairngorms. In 1954 the Commission's North Conservancy allowed free grazing upon 5,900 acres of higher ground in the Glenmore Forest Park, south of Loch Morlich, stretching up to the summits of Cairn Gorm and Cairn Lochain. The animals were permitted to graze freely like hill sheep. The enclosed area of Silver-mount continued to be used throughout.

The benefits of acquiring the higher ground of Silvermount and the surrounding unfenced pasture were immediate, as the reindeer could escape many of the flies and insects, helping to combat the problem of disease amongst them and the overall well-being of the herd was improved substantially. After a run of succesful calvings, confidence in the reindeer breeding experiment grew and by the end of 1956 The Department of Agriculture for Scotland recognised that the project had grown beyond an experimental stage: reindeer breeding in Scotland could take its place among local forms of livestock rearing.

Today Silvermount is the highest part of the fenced enclosure and we continue to lease the Northern slopes of the Cairngorm range, which have become central to the herd's development.

By the 1970's the herd had grown to a secure size, there were 69 reindeer in total and a number of 19 calves were born in the May of 1969.

Utsi Hut

In more recent years the hut was painted, in order to preserve the wood. Inside it still contains evidence of it's past use- a short sleeping platform, a table for keeping a journal, and a handcrafted birch stool.

In the early fifties, Mr Utsi built a small hut at the bottom of the enclosure of Silver Mount. He felt it was important to be 'on site' with the reindeer during the calving season as the reindeer calves were fragile when newly born, and access to the enclosure was a slow and rather arduous walk. The hut provided much needed relief and shelter from the Scottish weather and the resident midge. It contained a platform to sleep on, a table for keeping a journal and a small stool, all crafted by Mikel Utsi. The hut was used extensively throughout the 50's and 60's.

The hut was originally constructed from the wood of the crates within which some of the imported reindeer had been transported. It rested discreetly amongst the trees of the Caledonian pine forest.

'Road end camp', as it was known, marked the entrance into the enclosure, being the closest place to the access track until 1965, when a bridge was built to provide access from the ski road by way of the 'Sugar-bowl Trail'. Due to this, the herd became far more accessible.

The hut has had some repair work made to it, but still stands there to this day, much the same as it was when first built. It is not seen or used by many, but is treasured by those who do; is a mark of the herd's history and a reminder of the beginnings of the Cairngorm Reindeer herd.

Right: Road End Camp. Mikel Utsi uses a skin to provide some comfort for Sarek, who wears a traditional pack harness. Charles Ferguson, herder assists.
October 1955

REINDEER HOUSE

The herder's house of Glenmore

In August 1958 difficulties in repairing the road to Moormore cottage presented problems of access. The road and it's bridges had become dangerous to cars. The need arose for more suitable accomodation, closer to the new enclosures of Silvermount.

Mr Utsi and Dr Lindgren had approached the Forestry Commission in London for the approval of a building site in Glenmore for the Company's use. In the meantime, a formal sanction was made, whereby the reindeer herdsman could live at the Glenmore hostel. By 11th November 1959, the Company was finally offered a 25-year lease for a building in Glenmore, with a rent charge of £5 per annum.

The site measured 105' x 75' and was described by Dr Lindgren as *"undoubtably the best in Glenmore"*, placed against a green hill and not overlooked from any quarter. Mr Utsi signed the lease for the Company on the 13th January 1960. An Inverness architect had submitted drawings before Christmas which had already been carefully revised in view of the high building costs in northern Scotland. The plan for a stone-faced one story house, with room for a herdsman, an office and bedroom for the managing director and a well-lighted exhibition room for reindeer products at one end was put forward.

The building plans were approved by the Forestry Commission and by the Inverness County Council on condition that the house was stone-faced on three sides. Progress had been very slow, but by Christmas 1960, the grey-green slate roof was on.

Reindeer House with a view to Loch Morlich. The Glenmore forest
has since been repopulated.
July 1962
Photo: Vincent Utsi

The granite walls of Reindeer House remain unchanged to this day. The surrounding landscape has been changed significantly by the expanding Glenmore forest.
August 1963
Photo: B. Humble

The living room displaying 'reindeer artifacts', where Dr Lindgren and Mr Utsi would entertain their guests. It became 'The Shop' in 1989.
August 1961
Photo: B. Humble

From 18th August 1961 Reindeer House was officially open, providing "modern accommodation for reindeer herders, the managing director and a secretary, an office, and a well-lighted exhibition room, displaying reindeer products." All furniture and household equipment had been given or lent by Mr Utsi and his wife, and a telephone was installed in October.

The need to erect a 'pen' at Reindeer House, in which animals could be kept under observation or given treatment became urgent when the hand-reared calf 'Boko' refused to be left with the main herd and would follow Mr Utsi home. The Forestry Commission kindly leased a strip of land to the Company on the hillside immediately above Reindeer House. It was fenced in two sections, the larger adequate for segregating up to 30 members of the herd in the rut.

In February 1966 the plan for two bungalows to be built on the hill behind the Reindeer House was conveyed in a courteous letter from Inverness, which sought permission to change the shape and diminish the area of the reindeer pens. Mr Utsi replied that he had no objection, provided that an equivalent area could be fenced inside the adjacent wood, which was agreed.

Reindeer House, from which the herd could often be seen through binoculars, greatly facilitated the work on the reserve. The result of better organisation of visits to the reindeer were conspicuous even toward the end of the tourist season.

The benefits provided by the Reindeer Company's head quarters in Glenmore were immediate; more income could be made through organised visits to the herd than that which could be achieved through the selling of reindeer meat, as was the Company's initial aim. By the 1970's, the income achieved through visits to the reindeer had five times exceeded that which was brought in through the selling of skins and meat. Accounting records showed a steady incline in income from 'reindeer visits and exhibitions', compared with the unreliable and ever fluctuating demand for reindeer meat and skins.

A part of Mr Utsi's large collection of antlers was haphazardly displayed next to the main entrance.
August 1961
Photo: B. Humble

Today, Reindeer House, now know as, 'The Cairngorm Reindeer Centre' has undergone many changes and adaptations to it's first build.

It was designed and built specifically for the Reindeer Company to accommodate the herdsman and a secretary and can now house a work force of up to 8 people at any one time. All of the changes put upon it by the growing business, family and staff members can be seen today. The stone faced house is both a home and workplace full of character and history.

Predominantly made from granite, the building has stood the test of both time and weather; the walls have stood strong in the storms which have swept across the glen.

THE HILL TRIP

visiting the famous reindeer herd

Before main access to the herd was changed in 1965, visitors would walk to the mountains, following the herdsman through the Glenmore Forest. Here visitors stop to read a notice about the reindeer.
July 1958
Photo: O. Bjorkroth

Throughout the 60's and 70's, visits to see 'Mr Utsi and his famous reindeer' were increasingly popular. Mr Utsi was very sociable and made a memorable impression upon many of his visitors. He was often seen wearing elements of his traditional lappish dress. He had a colourful personality and was regarded by many as a "bit of a ladies' man" He was always delighted to 'show off' with his reindeer and is sometimes remembered more than the reindeer themselves.

Throughout the 70's, tours became more regular and the herders continued to take people onto the hill to find the reindeer. Donations were given in return for photos, and eventually a small fee was charged as a contribution to the herd's upkeep and management. Initially tours were arranged through the herder at Reindeer House by appointment only but by the late 60's the trips had become so frequent that at 11 O'clock every day, regardless of weather conditions, visitors could follow the herder onto the hill in search of the reindeer. The 'Hill Trip' had become a permanent fixture in the daily routine of the herdsman.

Mr Utsi feeds reindeer oxen 'Boy' whilst talking to a young family on the Visit.
August 1968

The '11 o'clock Hill Trip' was loved not only by the visitors to Reindeer House, but also by Mr Utsi, who was able to openly share his love of reindeer and his understanding of them with everybody he met. He would tell tales of his life in Lapland and reel off stories of his more comical reindeer exploits. He was extremely confident and friendly toward strangers, but often held a rather stern disposition around those working for him. To many who met him, he came across as completely eccentric. He enjoyed wearing his traditional Sami clothing on the visits, but loved and embraced Scottish cultures and other customs of Britain.

The British public were unfamiliar to reindeer and many had become more familiar with the fictions regarding reindeer than the facts. Even now, some still believe them to be fictional creatures. Today's Hill trip continues to be enjoyed by many. It provides a valuable learning experience for both the young and the old and gives everyone time to mingle and interact with the reindeer in their natural environment, whilst providing insight from the herders, who work continuously alongside them.

Since 1965 (when the access to the enclosure was changed) the hill trip has remained relatively unaltered. Trips still begin with the convoy of visitors in their cars, winding their way up the Ski road and leaving their vehicle at the car park. From here they 'follow the leader', walking along the Sugar-bowl trail, across the river and up again, passing through the main gate to the enclosure to see the feeding of the herd. When they are amongst the reindeer, people are often surprised by their small appearance, having imagined them to be larger like the native Red deer or perhaps their Scandinavian cousin, the moose.

The Scottish weather puts very few people off the Hill trip and despite wind, rain and snow visitors are enthused by the sight of the herd. The herder calls them from their grazing and the reindeer speed across, eager for an easy feed from a delighted visitor. During recent years visitors have been able to engage even more closely with the reindeer, by trekking with them into the Silvermount enclosure, from which they lead the reindeer down into the wild and undisturbed Caledonian Forest, re-discovering Utsi hut. From there, it is easy to imagine the beginnings of the herd in the 1950's when Mr Utsi led Sarek, his reindeer oxen, in search of other reindeer from his growing herd.

Clarke Hunter rides one of the reindeer oxen at the Käta by the reindeer Shelter. 1970's

Trekking with the reindeer Magnus and Bourbon. Robin and Anita Page enjoy a well earned rest on the top of Silver Mount, the highest point of the reindeer enclosure.
August 2012
Photo: Fiona Smith

The new ski road was opened to general traffic by 4th July, 1961, when about 80 persons, "most not equipped for the hills", were seen in the Cairngorm and Coire Cas area. By the Summer, the Glenmore camping site was packed and a steady stream of traffic went past to the large car park below Coire Cas. Here many families would leave their cars and walk into the mountains, often taking their unleashed dogs with them. Mr Utsi became increasingly concerned for his reindeer, as dog worrying had become a persistent problem; reindeer would often be found separated from the main herd, leading to losses among the young and vulnerable calves. The Forestry Comission had permitted the company to erect a sign asking visitors to "please keep dogs on leads".

THE REINDEER DON'T LIKE IT !

Dear Sir,
    I do not like dogs running loose on the Cairngorms. Some dogs chase anything. In the years that I have been introducing reindeer to Scotland many reindeer have been injured by dog worrying.
    The other thing I would like to suggest is that the new Cairngorm rangers should check that all hill walkers have a small shovel with them to dig down their dirt. There are no toilets on the hills, and reindeer are very clean animals.
    Yours Sincerely,
    Mikel Utsi.

Mr Utsi's letter placed in the Scots Magazine
September 1975

Signs were permitted by the Forestry Comission to warn walkers after attacks on the reindeer by loose dogs became a major concern.

Postcard from the '70's, showing the Ski road after it was first built, winding up to the car park below Cairngorm Mountain.
J. Arthur Dixon

"BRIDGING THE GAP TO THE REINDEER"

and a memorial stone for Mr Utsi

By 1975 Mr Utsi's health worsened. He frequently fell ill and subsequently spent more time resting at their home in Harston, Cambridge. His condition prevented him from making the short walk into the hills to see his reindeer on the mountains. This was what saddened him most during the latter part of his life.

He wrote a letter to future 'visitors to the herd', on Hospital stationary, from his hospital bed in Cambridge in 1975. The letter was postitioned outside Reindeer House for every visitor to read.

Sadly, he never fully recovered. His condition persisted over the subsequent years until he passed away in Cambridge on June 30th 1979 at the age of 71. He had become well liked and had made many friends during his 30 years in Britain. He was sorely missed by the great many who had come to know him.

He died leaving his wife, Dr Lindgren in charge of his beloved reindeer herd. She was helped by her family, including Vincent Utsi and her son John Lindgren, and the company shareholders. A new bridge to the reindeer herd was named Utsi Bridge in memory of her late husband.

Dear Visitors to the reindeer,

However much I might have wished to guide you, as before, to my dear reindeer, around which my thoughts are always circling, my health advisors have rescued me to this home of rest. I hope nevertheless that it will not be for too long a time. I am confident that if there is any where in the world that I can be restored, I am in that place.

Every morning, when you start driving up from Reindeer House, towards the reindeer in the hope of reaching them somewhere on the slopes of the Cairngorms, I think of you.

Yours devoted,

Mikel Utsi

Mr Utsi wrote this letter to all future visitors of his herd, when recovering in hospital.
This photo marks one of his last trips to his herd on the mountains.
Written 1975

The Scotsman   4th July 1979

MIKEL UTSI, the Laplander who brought reindeer back to Scotland after 800 years of extinction, has died in a Cambridge hospital at the age of 71.

Scores of tourists will remember tramping over the Cairngorms behind the colourful figure with the horn and red-tasselled cap, as he pointed out the deer and told their story. According to the Orkneyinga Saga, he would explain, red deer and reindeer were once hunted together by the Jarls of Orkney. They were never seen again for any length of time until one moonlit night in 1952 when he unloaded eight reindeer from his native Swedish Lapland on to the moors of Rothiemurchus.

He had spotted reindeer moss (a form of lichen) in the Cairngorms during a visit in 1947. Convinced that reindeer could thrive there, he and his wife, Dr Ethel Lindgren, helped form a Reindeer Council to supervise the experiment.

The first batch of animals from the Utsi family home lived on 300 acres of Rothiemurchus Forest leased by Lt.-Col. J. P. Grant to the newly-formed Reindeer Company, of which Mr Utsi was managing director. Later consignments went to the higher Glenmore Forest, leased by the North Conservancy, where there were fewer summer flies to worry the deer. The last import, from southern Norway, was in 1961, and the entire present herd of some 80 deer is Scottish-born.

Mr Utsi, who became a British subject in 1955, spent

SALLY MAGNUSSON

The man who brought back the reindeer

two-thirds of each year in the Cairngorms, where he built a stone bungalow at Glenmore called the Reindeer House. From there he could watch his herd moving on the distant hill. They were his babies: he knew each by name, tended them when they were sick, fed them, talked to them. When he transported any to the parks and zoos which clamoured for them, he would sleep with them in the van.

The deer also knew him. Lt.-Col. Grant describes the "battle of intellects" there used to be when Mr Utsi tried to lasso one of them. (He was a dab hand with a lasso). But once the halter was on, they were a team. Scores of children on holiday at Aviemore were treated to regular Christmas visits from a reindeer and sleigh and a jovial Mikel Utsi playing Santa.

It was his sense of fun that people will remember — the crinkly laugh, the leg-pulling, the endless fund of stories. He would tell, for instance, of the war years when he and a companion rescued hundreds of Norwegian refugees from the Germans in the mountainous Swedish borderland. He was more reticent about the decoration he won from King Haakon of Norway for these exploits.

"Quite a character" is how the people of Glenmore describe him, a born hunter who could find his way about the hills of his adopted Scotland with unerring ease. Stocky and weather-beaten, he was always a popular figure as he strode about in the colourful Lapp clothing that marked him out for miles.

Most of the gear he made himself — his boots from soft deerskin, his horn from antlers. Another trademark was his walking stick, cunningly hollowed to convert to a pipe. He was a craftsman, and the walls of Reindeer House are thick with evidence of his art —skins, carvings, ornaments.

But no mementoes of Mikel Utsi speak as eloquently as the presence in the Cairngorms of the reindeer he fostered and whose interests he continued to manage by telephone from his hospital bed right up to 36 hours before he died after four years of illness.

Mr William Brotherston, a director of the Reindeer Company, said yesterday he hoped Mr Utsi's work would now be expanded. "His was a remarkable venture. Now it should go further."

Reindeer expert dies aged 71

A Harston man who proved that reindeer could live and breed in Scotland has died at the age of 71.

Mr Mikel Utsi was born and brought up in a well known reindeer - breeding family in Sweden before coming to Britain in 1947 to start his Scottish experiment.

A Fellow of the Royal Anthropological Institute, he lived at Sunbourn, Newton Mill, Harston, with his anthropologist wife, Dr E. J. Lindgren.

With Dr H. M. Dott, of the animal Research Station in Huntingdon Road, Cambridge, he did much research into reindeer breeding, especially artificial insemination techniques.

Mr Utsi became a British citizen after directing refugee release operations along the Norway frontier during the Second World War.

He leaves one child and his wife, who plans to continue his work.

Cambridge Evening News
3rd July 1979

" Mikel has proved what can be done in re-establishing reindeer in Scotland, thereby and incidentally creating countless friends and admirers.... "

Extract taken from Colonel Croft's letter
to Dr Lindgren
2nd July 1979

"
These hills will not be quite the same without him somehow, and the valley too will 'feel' different - as with the felling of some great tree.
"

Quoted at Mr Utsi's funeral from a letter written to Dr
Lindgren by Roger O'Donovan,
Vice Principal of Glenmore Lodge.

9th July 1979

Extract from Dundee Courier & Advertiser

"Thanks to 50 senior apprentices from H.M.S. Caledonia, Rosyth, the public will soon have access to an area in the Cairngorms, where reindeer have been introduced and are now breeding.

The apprentices will set out this morning to build a bridge over the Allt Mor River gorge, about 3 1/2 miles south of Glenmore Lodge. The planning and construction has been left entirely to the apprentices as part of a leadership course.

They will camp on the site 'till Friday, when it is expected the bridge will be completed.

The main structure will consist of four 45-foot pine trees secured on supports. A walkway of planks will be laid on top of the logs and handrails will be fitted.

The trees, each weighing about a third of a ton, have been provided by the Forestry Commission.

Two old cars:

The most difficult part of the operation will be transporting the trees over 3 1/2 miles of rough country. The apprentices have stripped down two old cars and adapted them for this purpose.

Last Spring apprentices from H.M.S Caledonia built a bridge at Loch Errochty, in North Perthshire, and in the summer, a mountain shelter near Loch Avon, in the Cairngorms."

Above: The 'temporary bridge' assembled from parts of the original structure was replaced in 1979 by the 'Utsi bridge', which still stands today.
Photo: Vincent Utsi

Bridge to reindeer herd nearly ready

A GROUP of 40 volunteers have given up their holidays to construct a new bridge across the burn leading to the famous herd of reindeer near Sugarbowl Hill in the Cairngorms.

The volunteers from the Officers Training Corps, of Edinburgh, Herlot-Watt, Glasgow and Strathclyde universities, look at completing the project at the weekend, two weeks after they started.

The last bridge was destroyed last year, when parts of it were washed away in a freak thunderstorm. Since then, visitors wanting to view the reindeer have had to totter precariously across a make-shift bridge to reach the spot.

Every summer visitors, many from overseas, are led by a herdsman down a ravine, across a burn and up a steep climb to see the herd of about 100 reindeer.

The volunteers, including eight girls, are being supervised by two Royal Engineers, and are camping near the site.

'The Press and Journal' 27th July 1979

The "substantial new foot bridge" over the Allt Mhor burn had been built by the Edinburgh and Heriot Watt Universities' Officers Training Corps and was completed on the 26th July 1979.

Herder, Jonathan Pott smashes a bottle of champagne against the newly built bridge on the day of it's completion. It is named "Utsi bridge" by Dr Lindgren as a tribute to her husband. The volunteers who helped to construct it watch from above.
26th July 1979

The cows and calves cross the bridge for their first time. The bridge has survived for 33 years. It is estimated that 25,000 human feet and 464 reindeer hooves cross the bridge each year.

Wanted: Reindeer keeper in Cairngorms

A NEW keeper is required to look after Scotland's only herd of reindeer in the Cairngorms.

MR UTSI 'S REINDEER HERDERS

Turning an experiment into a success

THE REINDEER COMPANY LIMITED

REINDEER   RESERVE   ROUTINE

in the absence of Mr Utsi

originally drafted in 1971

(Instructions, brought up-to-date in June 1978)

(1) Before leaving Reindeer House in the morning, spy out the nearest slopes carefully with field-glasses.

(2) Leave Reindeer House for checking the herd at 9 a.m., or, if you are taking Visitors up, at 11a.m. If reindeer are missing, someone should go up earlier.

(3) Each person doing reindeer work must carry a raincoat or other water-proof clothing, a haversack containing a bag with about 3 lb. of supplementary fodder, in the correct mixture (more, if the reindeer are fenced it); one packet of Ryvita; a reindeer halter; and his own picnic lunch, preferably with thermos. A walking stick is also always useful. A sharp knife is required if a reindeer has died on the hill, for skinning.

(4) An eye should be kept on the herd until most people have come down from the hills; and someone must be within reach of the reindeer until 5.30 p.m. in case a dog attacks them, or people worry the calves. (Hours are of course longer in the calving season). If the reindeer are all right, fences should be carefully checked for weak spots.

(5) The reindeer should be kept out of sight of the Ski Road, Ski car park and Ski lift and for that reason should not be fed with the mixture or Ryvita on or near that area!

(6) If there are loose dogs about, the owner must be warned to keep the dog on a lead. One can mention small calves in the herd or other special circumstances. If no owner can be found the dog must be taken down to Reindeer House and reported to the Forester, to the Police, or both.

(7) Visitors who are good walkers and are suitably equipped for the hill can be taken up for payment, but not people unfit, too old, or too young.

Old or young can come as far as the Käta Shelter in the East End to visit the nearest reindeer. Payment at the gate. No dogs inside the reindeer enclosures.
Salt licks should always be put out when the reindeer are f

Mr Peter Voy sitting at the bonfire
beside the turf hut lappish Käta. The
reindeer nearest Peter is Lad
13th December 1977.
Photo: Colin Davey

M. N. P. UTSI

25 June 1978

1950's

From the early 50's, Mikel Utsi had sought help in caring for the reindeer and helping them to become established in Scotland. Initially he received much of the help from his extended Sami family in Sweden. He began 'training' local herders soon after. He found there were plenty of men who would gladly assist him. The work was hard, the reindeer mortality rate was high, and as such there was a lot of pressure on the main herders to maintain the welfare of Mr Utsi's reindeer. The job, though full of excitement and originality, was extremely tough and offered few home comforts.

In the early years of establishing the herd, help was given firstly by Nicolaus Labba, a cousin of Mikel's from northern Sweden. Mr Kenneth MacLennan assisted in 1956 and, upon his leave , Charles Ferguson, a school leaver from Aviemore, took over the main duties.

Much of the work involved an extensive amount of fencing, both at the original reserve of Moormore and then later also at the enclosure of Silvermount. Volunteer helpers came in 1958; Mr J. Bedford, a veterinary student from Cambridge stayed at Moomore cottage for a month, Mr R Barton Park for some days in the calving season and Mr Hillar Kallas for a month in August. Mr Edwin Wakeling came as a supplementary herder in 1959. He was a nurseryman from Kent and knew the area well from hiking holidays. He was very systematic and his approach to the work was admired by Mr Utsi and Dr Lindgren. He established a diary for recording the individual movements in the herd and could recognise the reindeer by name. In April 1958 Charles Ferguson left his position as herder and Mr Wakeling took this permanent post.

Mr A. F. Montgomery of the Outward Bound Sea School stayed at Moormore cottage during Mr Wakeling's holidays and occasional help was given by Mr Lindsay of the Glenmore shop.

Left: Alan Smith herds the reindeer towards the hill enclosure.
1980
Photo: Robert Seymour

Right: Charles Ferguson with yearling female, 'Noki' in the lower corral, not far from Road End Camp.
30th Sept 1955
Photo: A. Whittington

1960's

Mr Edwin C Wakeling continued as sole reindeer herdsman throughout the year of 1960, supervised by Mr Utsi. Wakeling's diary had become an increasingly useful source of information on the herd and Wakeling maintained a steady routine.

Some assistance had been provided by his brother Derek. 'Tommy' Mackenzie, a local forestry worker and Mr John Ward, a London school teacher, also helped Mr Wakeling. Vincent Utsi, Mikel's son stayed for the Summer at Moormore Cottage or in the Forester's House in Glenmore. He learned various reindeer techniques and lent a hand where needed on the reserve.

With the completion of Reindeer House in 1961, Edwin Wakeling was the first herder to take up residence there, but he left shortly after marrying a local girl and took up forestry work in a nearby glen. Several people put themselves forward for the vacant position which was left open, while Vincent Utsi proved an invaluable help on the reserve in July and August 1961. Mr Utsi spent the majority of his time with the herd until a more permanent replacement for Mr Wakeling could be found. Dr Lindgren and Miss Ragnhild Andreassen kept house at Moormore cottage for most of the year.

Extract from the Reindeer Company reports, 1962:

" *Experience over ten years had shown that there was no shortage in Britain of men, both young and middle aged, who were keen to try reindeer herding, and of these a number found the life congenial. Training them beyond an elementary stage was not easy, however, and it was increasingly difficult to establish habits which could be relied upon in Mr Utsi's absence.*"

"*The new conditions of Glenmore were complex and shifting, a complete contrast to the isolation, in spartan surroundings, which Nicolaus Labba had loyally survived at Moormore in 1952 and 1953. The route of the 55,000 persons said to have used the chairlift up Cairngorm from its inauguration in December, 1961 to May 1962, and the thousands of cars which travelled up the ski road, bisected the reindeer pasture, on the western side of which part of the reindeer herd now often grazed. Any "reindeer herder" was regarded by the visitors as a romantic figure and temptations abounded to tarry near the Ski road, beside the car park milk bar or in the snack cafe of the new high Sheiling. Skiers from the region's far flung hostels and boarding houses, military men in training, Glenmore lodge students on courses, youth hostellers in the former Glenmore lodge, hikers housed in two large local barracks, caravan and tent-dwellers on the large camp-site ,tourists up for the day, the Forestry Commission staff and their personal guests and they were always included some who wished to see and question the reindeer herder, photograph the herd, call (or if possible stay) at Reindeer House, and invite the herder to drinks and entertainments. To subordinate such demands and distractions to routine maintenance, even to urgent reindeer tasks, was a stringent test of character and discipline.*"

Vincent Utsi continued to assist his father when he was available. He attended a Swedish school, so his time helping was always throughout the summer. Many who did help did not stay long; they often tired of the long distances of ground which had to be covered on foot to find stray reindeer.

The Company made no charge for the use of Reindeer House, but adult herders contributed £10 per week towards the cost of light, heat, warm water and the cooker.

From mid August 1966 Mr Utsi recieved herding assistance from his nephew Per Ola Utsi (a Bantam weight lifting champion of Sweden) who had travelled from Porjus after hearing of his uncle's illness in May. During this time a large number of replies to the post, advertised in the local papers were answered and interviews were arranged by Dr Lindgren.

Right: Edwin Wakeling with
reindeer calf, 'Per'.
25th September 1958
Photo: Alex C. Cooper

Left: Roger Anderson of Glasgow,
leading Charles the reindeer ox.
26th December 1968
Photo: Scottish Sunday Express

1970's

By the mid Seventies Mikel Utsi had become seriously ill; the physically demanding work was wearing heavily on his health. His visits to his beloved reindeer on the hill became far less frequent and sadly for him, they eventually stopped alltogether. The Company was in desperate need of a more reliable and permanent herdsman to relieve Mr Utsi of the management of the herd.

Mr Thomas Matheson continued his assistance to the Utsis and was helped during school holidays by young and eager volunteers Roger Anderson of Glasgow and local lad, Ewan Mackenzie, son of a former mountain rescue leader. They began to show talent by the spring of 1970 and were considered *"a welcome standby"* by Mr Utsi.

The son of a retired army major, Jonathan Pott, applied and fulfilled the position of herder for 9 months in '73 and '74. He was very capable, and quickly devised a system for identifying reindeer. He left briefly to resume his studies but had suggested that he would like to return to the position for a further 2 years after his studies were completed. Mr Utsi welcomed him back and he commenced his work as a full time herder in August 1975.

1976 was a record breaking summer for all of Britain. Temperatures soared and the reindeer had to endure one of the hottest summers on record. The herd incurred inevitable losses due to the unorthodox weather. Mr Utsi, frustrated by his failing health and his inability to be more directly involved with the herd, had asked Jonathan if he would be interested in purchasing it from him. Jonathan seemed like the ideal candidate to take over from Mr Utsi; he was young, keen, able and extremely fond of the reindeer, whom he had come to know so well. He took the offer very seriously and negotiations between them began.

After much time passed, it became clear that no agreement could be met about the Company's assets and valuations. Some thought it unlikely that Mr Utsi would ever have been able to 'give up' his beloved reindeer herd whilst still alive and that he was unwilling to relinquish control of the reindeer whom he had dedicated so much of his life to.

Mr Pott, despite his obvious love for the reindeer, wrote and informed Mr Utsi that he did not wish to continue as Keeper and so his employment ended on the 26th August 1977. Once again, The Reindeer Company began the search for yet another keeper. More advertisements were placed in the local papers and many candidates applied. The post was filled by a promising young man who came with an excellent reference, Mr Peter Voy. He worked well and was keen, but he left after a year to complete his studies at Aberdeen University. Once again the vacant post was advertised in the regional press and by 1979 David Burkitt was employed as Head Keeper. 18 year old Alan Smith, the son of a gamekeeper from Allt na Breac, Caithness, worked alongside him in his first few months. Shortly after Alan's arrival, Mr Utsi passed away in Cambridge on the 30th June 1979, leaving his wife Dr Lindgren solely in charge. She became more directly involved in the management of the herd, and was kept up to date regularly by the herders. She never managed the walk onto the hill. Dave Burkitt departed just 3 months after he had started and Jonathan Pott returned again to join Alan Smith for the summer months and for much of that year.

Alan spent an increasing amount of time out in the mountains with some of the more far-ranging reindeer, as well as completing the routine tasks of feeding the enclosed reindeer and leading the daily visits. He reported regularly to Dr Lindgren via the telephone, as she often stayed at her home in Cambridge. She visited Reindeer House frequently for short spells which kept those living at Reindeer House in a constant state of alert. She was very trusting of Alan and awarded him free reign much of the time to make important decisions about the management of the herd. She respected him greatly for his care of the reindeer and admired his initiative. It was clear that she thought him to be a worthy keeper to follow on from her late husband.

Right: Jonathan Pott feeding
the herd in the Summer time.
Photo: Perry McIntyre

1980's

After the death of Mr Utsi, the young herder, Alan Smith, who had just turned 19, was kept on as Keeper for Dr Lindgren. Jonathan Pott guided him for his first 3 months and Vincent Utsi, who had replaced his father's position of Managing Director, was unable to spend a great deal of time there. Alan frequently had to fathom out for himself how to best care for the roaming herd of reindeer.

His daily work included guiding visitors onto the hill to see the reindeer and walking deep into the heart of the Cairngorms in search of strays, retrieving them and treating them for any veterinary problems. Dr Lindgren relied heavily on Alan to continue where Mr Utsi had left off. He reported to her daily with accounts of the herd and though she did not think much for his record keeping and administrative skills, she admired his dedication; in just a short time, he had learnt all the reindeer by name, observed their characteristics closely and showed great concern for their well being. Dr Lindgren recruited volunteers from all walks of life to assist Alan.

Alan 19 years old, gathering
'freerangers' from the high tops.
Summer 1979
Photo: David Burkitt

CLAUS ENCOUNTERS OF A REINDEER MAN

DAVID MANSELL

Ranger Alan Smith among Britain's only herd of reindeer, now grazing in the Cairngorms. Reintroduced to Scotland from Lapland after an 800-year absence, they recently starred in the film 'Santa Claus: The Movie.'

Observer
15th December 1985

NEW OWNERS FOR THE HERD

'Under new management'

In June 1981, Elizabeth Dansie, 'Tilly', travelled up from her family home in Hertfordshire to volunteer with the reindeer after having completed her degree in Zoology. She learnt a lot about the reindeer and enjoyed working with Alan, but Dr Lindgren disliked the nature of Alan and Tilly's relationship, fearing that her keeper might be distracted by the English girl. She was glad, therefore, when Tilly left for Sweden to take part in a project to radio-track moose in 1982. She returned, however, to the Cairngorms and to Alan in May 1983. Dr Lindgren was relieved to find that Tilly had no intention on leaving the herd, or the keeper, and the couple were married in July of that year.

They continued to live at Reindeer House and became a capable team, managing all aspects of the business. Tilly helped greatly, both with the reindeer and down at the house, having a strong handle on the secretarial work, which allowed Alan to spend more time with the reindeer. In 1985 they had their first child, Alex, and a year later their second child, Fiona, was born.

On the 23rd March 1988, Dr Lindgren died at Reindeer House at the age of 83. She was the major shareholder, Director and Secretary of The Reindeer Co. Ltd. Her shares were inherited by her son John Lindgren and Mr Utsi's son Vincent Utsi who continued to run the Company for 1 ½ years, during this time they decided to sell the Reindeer Company and actively encouraged the Keeper and his wife to make them an offer. Alan and Tilly were both very dedicated to the reindeer, and gathered funds to buy the herd. Vincent Utsi remarked at the time that "The experiment to introduce a herd of reindeer to the Scottish Highlands could be considered a success, since a local family are now prepared to purchase the company". On 4th August 1989 Mr and Mrs A. J. Smith officially became the new owners of Britain's only herd of reindeer.

Above: New owners of the herd, Alan and
Tilly, transformed Reindeer House into a
Visitor Centre and erected the sign outside
Reindeer House.
4th August 1989
Photo: Laurie Campbell

Left: The Smith family, photographed with
the reindeer and sleigh. Alex and Fiona
have grown up with reindeer and are closely
involved with the herd today. Reindeer
Parsley and Miligan stand amongst them.
October 1994
Photo: Laurie Campbell

1990's

Alan and Tilly opened up the west door at Reindeer House so that the room, which had been Dr Lindgren's drawing room for entertaining her guests, became the reception area and shop for the newly named 'Cairngorm Reindeer Centre'. The 11 O'clock visit was continued and in addition a second visit at 2:30 pm and a third at 4pm were arranged. The reindeer paddocks behind the house were transformed into a small exhibition area which was open to the public.

Over the following years, the interior of Reindeer House was adapted to accommodate the young family, the volunteers and the visitors to the Centre. The attic was converted, adding two bedrooms, and the interior wall dividing the kitchen and living room was demolished . All the work was done by Alan Smith and much help was given to him by Scott Nicol and Mark Francis, 'Beads'. Tilly concentrated her efforts on the running of The Centre, the visits, the office work and the shop.

In the hill enclosure, the old reindeer shelter, which acted as a corral for the reindeer, had become dilapidated and so was rebuilt early in the summer of 1990. With no road access to the enclosure, they put in place a wire, which crossed the ravine of the Allt Mhor burn, to transport the materials needed.

Above: The 'old reindeer shelter' in the hill enclosure needed replacing.
May 1990

Right: Scott, Alex and Fiona enjoying the demolition of the old shelter.
May 1990

The reindeer paddocks officially opened to the public on the 4th August 1989. In October 2001 the area was extended to incorporate the adjacent woodland.
Photo: Alex Smith

The fence to the Silvermount enclosure was in dire need of repair so in the August of 1990 a helicopter was hired to fly in fencing materials to rebuild the perimeter fence. Other old fences were replaced by new ones and internal fences were realigned. In total 1,000 metres of fencing were repaired or replaced. 500 metres of wooden walkways were constructed within the enclosure to protect the ground from the increasing numbers of visitors.

At the beginning of the 1990's, the main income was generated from visits to the reindeer, the Reindeer Shop, the rising numbers of Christmas events, and the new 'Reindeer Support Scheme'. The scheme allowed visitors and supporters of the herd to 'adopt' individual reindeer.
By 1995 The Reindeer Centre had settled into a successful and steady business and was able to employ staff in addition to having seasonal voluntary help.
In 2001 Britain saw its first major outbreak of foot-and-mouth since 1969. The implications were that severe restrictions on animal movements were put in place. Many areas of the British countryside were 'off limits' to the general public to prevent the spread of the highly contagious disease. Much of the Highlands of Scotland were unaffected, so hill walkers continued unrestricted into the Cairngorm mountains where the reindeer roamed. Fearing the risks to the herd of infection, Alan and Tilly felt it was in their best interest to bring all the reindeer into the 1,000 acre hill enclosure and, for the first time, close the Centre in Glenmore and deny access to the public.
With no visitors for 6 months, The Reindeer Support Scheme, which had been in place for 5 years, gave crucial support towards the upkeep of the herd during a time of much uncertainty.

The members who form The Reindeer Support Scheme have over many years proved to be fundamental to the continuation of the herd. Now in it's 22nd year it includes over 1000 reindeer adopters from across the UK and world wide.

Certificates and letters to reindeer supporters over the years. The Reindeer Support Scheme is still growing, and was of critical importance to the economic survival of the herd at the time of the foot and mouth outbreak, 2001.

Grounded

Picture: MIKE SCOTT

In the cold: Alan and Tilly Smith feed the reindeer that Father Christmas will use for deliveries this year, but only in Scotland

The outbreak of foot-and-mouth was detrimental to the Company's finances and caused much worry and uncertainty about the herd's future. Article from the Daily Telegraph. The photograph is of Tilly feeding reindeer, Trebor.
Article: Robin Page
Photo:Mike Scott
November 2001

Foot and mouth means Father Christmas will be unable to use his reindeer to help with deliveries in England and Wales this year, says **Robin Page**

Oh dear, poor Father Christmas. This festive season is going to be a very trying time for the old boy. This year, he has to cover the whole of England and Wales by bike. Everywhere else, he is free to fly with his beloved reindeer and sleigh; but here in England, he has been grounded.

Every year for the British leg of his deliveries, Father Christmas and his friend, Rudolph, use the animals at the Reindeer Centre at Glenmore, situated at the foot of the Cairngorm Mountains. There, Alan and Tilly Smith look after Britain's only herd of almost wild, breeding reindeer. But for foot and mouth restrictions, those animals would set off once again to add their brand of Christmas magic of Christmas to thousands of children.

In previous years, excited children have flocked to see the teams of reindeer as they visited all parts of Britain, from the portals of Harrods to the shopping centre at Wigan, via the old cowshed in my farmyard.

Whereas the Scottish Agricultural Department has given Rudolph special dispensation to travel around Scotland for the Christmas season, Defra evidently believes that reindeer can spread foot and mouth – an interesting fact in itself.

It is true that reindeer have cloven hooves and so can get foot and mouth, in theory, yet, whenever I have spoken to Defra about the possibility of wild deer spreading foot and mouth during the current epidemic, it has dismissed the idea.

So if wild deer in Devon and Cumbria have played no part in spreading foot and mouth, and only a proper public inquiry will tell us otherwise, why does Defra believe that strictly supervised and monitored reindeer will now spread foot and mouth?

The truth is that for most of the year, the Cairngorm reindeer live almost as wild animals in two herds: one in the Cairngorms and one in the nearby Cromdale Hills. Because of their specialised diet of heather, mosses and lichens, they do not share their grazing and browsing with other animals, apart from wild red deer and roe.

Once with Father Christmas, they ride in comfort and luxury in roomy lorries and their chances of infection are precisely nil. When stopping for rest and recreation at our farm, the reindeer do not mix with our cattle and in any case, we are in a disease-free area. Yet according to Defra, the Cairngorm reindeer would have to travel in a disinfected and sealed lorry for every journey.

The seal could be broken only by a vet and once one journey had been undertaken, the animals would have to be in quarantine for 21 days. Consequently, if the reindeer visited Harrods, they would have to be housed at Harrods for 21 days and, of course, moss and heather do not grow in Central London.

Normally, the visits of Father Christmas and his reindeer to shopping centres in Britain supply Tilly and Alan with their main source of income, which allows them to maintain the herd for the rest of the year.

Determined not to be outdone by Defra, Alan, Tilly and their reindeer can be seen at the Cairngorm Reindeer Centre from 10am–5pm until tomorrow, at a special event called Christmas Fun (admission £3). Call 01479 861228 for details. Father Christmas will be on duty too, because he will be training for his great bike ride early in the morning. Rudolph and his friends wish everybody a Happy Christmas, wherever you are.

Since 1990, The Cairngorm Reindeer Herd has been split between two sites; Cairngorm and Glenlivet. Establishing the herd at a new site reduced the grazing pressures on the Cairngorms which allowed numbers of the herd to increase and helped to secure the overall future of the reindeer in Scotland.

The move to Glenlivet, in particular the Cromdale hills, which stretch out to the north of the National park and reach heights of over 700m, has been extremely important. Up on the high ground, there grows an abundance of lichen, making this a prime grazing site, specifically for the winter. In 1998, the new land was particularly useful as the breeding of that year was controlled; for some of the cows, contact to the bull was limited, because the herd was split across the two sites.

The site in Glenlivet has proved to be a necessary part of the reindeer pasture. It has become the reindeer's 'second home' and is also a safeguard against the spread of contagious and transmittable diseases such as foot-and-mouth and the blue-tongue virus.

Reindeer bull, Utsi, grazing the plentiful lichens of the Cromdale hills.
October 2003
Photo: Nigel Housden

Since 1990 some of the herd spend the winter months on the Cromdale hills, to the north of the
Cairngorm range, where there is an abundance of natural grazing.
February 2012
Photo: Alex Smith

2000's to 2012's

In 1993 Alan and Tilly were invited to attend the first International Festival of the World Reindeer Herders. People from all over the 'reindeer world' gathered in Tromso for the first ever international festival of its kind. It gave Tilly and Alan great insight into the status of reindeer and the lives of those who rely upon them, throughout the Northern Hemisphere. They met a large number of people actively involved in reindeer husbandry, and it was perhaps this meeting with other reindeer cultures that helped inspire Tilly to write a book about her own rather unique family life with the reindeer. She completed the book 'Velvet Antlers and Velvet Noses' which was published in 1995.

In 2005 Tilly and Alan visited the 400th Winter Market in Jokkmokk, Northern Sweden and within the same year Tilly travelled to Outer Mongolia to visit the Tsataan reindeer people. The trip was an arduous one, and they took several days riding on horseback, whilst being followed by wolves, to reach the camp. The Tsataan family that they stayed with were friendly and the reindeer were incredibly tame. Tilly wrote about her travel there extensively in her second book, 'The Real Rudolph', which explores the natural history of the reindeer.

Toward the end of the winter of 2009, Alex Smith travelled to Kautakeino in the north of Norway to attend the 4th World Reindeer Herders' Congress, to represent the Scottish herd. The congress takes place every four years and is hosted in reindeer herding regions across the world. At the congress reindeer people and indigenous groups are able to discuss global and political issues together, which affect and unite them all. The next congress is to be held in Genhe, in the north easterly forests of China to visit the Aoluguy, a group of Evekni reindeer herding people.

Left: Tilly and her son Alex travel to
Mongolia to visit the Tsataan people.
Inspired, Tilly wrote her second book,
'The Real Rudolph'
March 2005
Photo: Alex Smith

Far Left: One-and-a-half reindeer
families. Tilly and Alex Smith
photographed with the Tsataan family.
2005
Photo: Jess Warner

REINDEER OXEN AND CHRISTMAS

'Tis the season to be jolly- busy!'

Sleigh Pullers

Reindeer oxen have been used throughout history as beasts of burden, capable of carrying weights of up to 33 kilos and pulling up to twice their own body weight (approximately 250 kilos). The practice of castrating male reindeer has been in place for thousands of years, and is still an important part of reindeer husbandry across the northern world. Domestication of reindeer began long ago in the upper palaeolithic era, often referred to as 'the age of the reindeer'. It was a time when man relied heavily upon them as a source of food and clothing. Cave paintings as far south as Altamira in Spain show the earliest evidence of reindeer and man together. The youngest of these paintings are thought to be 11,000 years old.

Over two thirds of the world's population of domesticated reindeer live within Russia where there are approximately 16 groups of indigenous people whose cultures are centred around the reindeer. It was in Southern Siberia where scientists believe reindeer were first domesticated 7,000 years ago. Since then, indigenous people such as the Evenki people, the Tsataan and Dolgans, all of whom ride their reindeer, have lived alongside them and rely upon them for food and clothing. Their ancestors began using reindeer as draught animals for over 2,000 years. By castrating the reindeer bulls they produced a more docile, workable animal, suitable for riding, packing and harnessing to a sledge. In the Chinese 'Chronicles of the Liang Dynasty', dating between 629 and 636, Yao Silian wrote of people living in the northern forests, who "kept deer instead of cattle and used them to pull carriages". A later publication, the 'New book of the Tang Dynasty', gives more detailed reference to the tribe of Ju who lived to the north of Lake Baikal and used deer to pull 'carriages'.

The Sami people use their reindeer oxen as draught animals, harnessing and attaching them to sledges to transport people, food, and materials for making camps. The reindeer oxen were crucial to their traditionally nomadic way of life. Domesticated reindeer, oxen in particular, have been used by man for over 2,000 years.

Above: "Going to the reindeer festival."
A lino-cut by the Yakut artist A. P. Munkalov.
1965

Right: An ederly Nenets woman drives a train of reindeer sleds across the summer tundra. Yamal Paninsula, Siberia, Russia.
Photo: Brian & Cherry Alexander

Christmas Reindeer

The association between Christmas and reindeer came after the year 1827, when Clement C. Moore, wrote his famous poem 'Twas the Night Before Christmas'. He was an expert in folk-law and his poem blended aspects of many legends, including; St Nicolas, the patron saint of travel, and the Dutch equivalent Sinterklaas, the pagan Midwinter Festival of Yule, whose feasts and activities traditionally are used to appease the gods, and Odin, the warrior god of wisdom and war from Norse mythology, who rode an eight legged horse distributing rewards or punishments to the Norse people. It is thought that these ancient stories could have inspired Moore, but regardless of his reasonings, the poem became a huge success in America and it's popularity spread from there. Now, the story of Santa Claus and his eight reindeer is a Christmas tradition in its own right.

An illustration of the eight reindeer from Clement C. Moore's famous poem 'Twas the night before Christmas':
"...he whistled, and shouted, and called them by name: "Now Dasher, now! Dancer, now! Prancer and Vixen,
On! Comet, on! Cupid, on! Donder and Blitzen..."

In Scotland, Mikel Utsi had his own uses for his reindeer oxen. He depended heavily upon 'Sarek', the only oxen brought to Scotland from his own herd in Sweden. Sarek was tame, easily caught and the other reindeer followed him well. Mr Utsi would place the pack harness onto the reindeer and lead him out from the enclosure in search of straying reindeer grazing on the open pasture, to lead them back to the main herd.

Cairn Lochan Safari with Mikel Utsi, Sarek (carrying pack) and Kirtik.
8th August 1956
Photo: Mr Een

Mr Utsi, passionate about his Sami way of life, continued to use his reindeer oxen in traditional ways, haltering and harnessing them, and using them to pull sledges. He took his reindeer to local towns for the summer shows and for Christmas festivities. His first visit to Aviemore at Christmas was in 1952 for a children's party.

Lochan na Beinne

Coire Laogh Mor

Coire na Ciste car park
(not yet there)

Coire na Ciste

An t-Aonach
"windy ridge"

Reindeer sledging in the Cairngorms with friends, with a view of the Cairngorms and reindeer pasturage behind.
Mikel Utsi and Miss McGeagh, with Sarek pulling Charles Ferguson in the sled.

Vikhta and Boko
visit the Strathspey
Farmers' Club Show,
Grantown.
8th August 1963
Photo: Moray and
Nairn Newspaper.

Vikhta pulls Mr Utsi's
wheel adapted sled
past the Glenmore
campsite.
31st October 1965
Photo: E. S. Bone

Kirtik demonstrates the wearing of a pack harness at the Grantown Show.
6th August 1959
Photo: E. J. Lindgren

Mikel Utsi takes a break whilst training reindeer cow Anite (left) and ox Vikhta (right) in Glenmore. He adapted a sledge by
adding wheels to combat the problems of having little or no snow.
31st October 1965
Photo: E. S. Bone

Aviemore Children's Party. (From left to right) Vincent Utsi, Mr Mutch, Mr Utsi, Mr Loban, Alistar Scott, Douglas Fraser, Maria Matlak, Janette Robertson, Caroline MacBean, Fraser Stewart, Janette MacBean, Alan Ross, Charles Haggerty, John Garrow. Standing top right: Mr L Mesurier. The reindeer are Sarek and Per.

24th December 1959

Photo: Aberdeen Journals

By the time Alan and Tilly Smith had taken over the running of the herd, there were fifteen trained reindeer oxen and they had begun venturing to further towns in Scotland with teams consisting of, four reindeer oxen, two calves, and a sleigh. They also visited hospitals and homes for charity events.

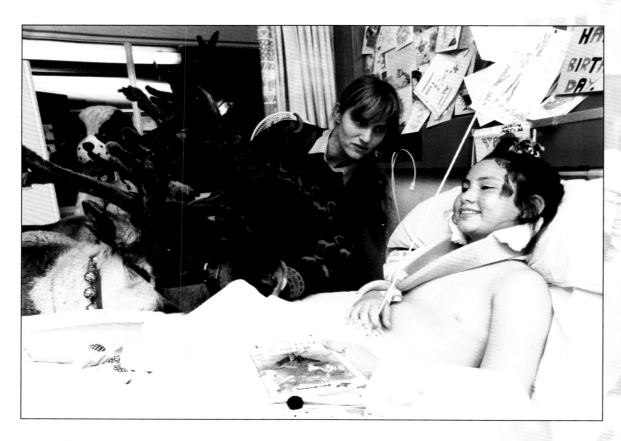

Above: Keith, a Christmas Reindeer, visits the
children's ward in Harrow Hospital.
November 1993
Photo: Ian Turner

Background: Alan Smith at a Christmas parade,
The Mound, Edinburgh.
November 1987
Photo: Stuart Guild

From the late 1970's local 'Christmas events' were becoming regular, but only took place within Scotland. It was not until the 1990's that these events reached England. One of the first Christmas events in England took place at the King Edward Court in Windsor on the 9th December 1993. The Cairngorm Reindeer have visited the world famous Harrods department store since 1997, traditionally beginning every 'Christmas tour' there on the first weekend of November.

Harrods owner Mohamed Al Fayed in an earlier festive scene. The reindeer are real

Mohamed Al Fayed meeting the Cairngorm Reindeer during the Harrods' Christmas parade, London.
December 2000
Clipping: Choice Magazine

DAILY EXPRESS

THURSDAY DECEMBER 24 1959

3 a.m. forecast: Sun and showers

A card from Giles and the Express

'Christmas Reindeer in Britain'. This cartoon by 'Giles'
featured in the Daily Express 1959.

The most northerly Christmas event took place in 1992 in the town of Thurso, in the north of Scotland. In 1999 the reindeer travelled to Ballymena, Northern Ireland for their most westerly event, and their most easterly event took place in 2002 in Great Yarmouth, Norfolk. The southernmost town that the reindeer have visited is Truro, Cornwall, in 2006. On each tour, any team of reindeer and their herders could be away from their home for anytime up to 2 weeks, so the Company have adopted a network of 'bases' across the UK. These places, suitable to use as temporary 'reindeer and herder' accommodation help to make long journeys such as the 630 mile trip to Truro possible by providing overnight rest-stops along the way.

Today, the herd includes approximately 50 oxen- "Christmas reindeer"- which are all trained to harness, both for trekking and for pulling sledges and they have become an integral part of the herd. The reindeer oxen bring great delight to the public both at home and 'on tour' and help to improve public awareness of The Cairngorm Herd. They promote tourism to their home in the Highlands and the financial rewards of their work across the country helps toward the herd's upkeep for the rest of the year.

Once Christmas has passed and 'all the little girls and boys' across the world have received their 'visit from St Nick', the Christmas reindeer can rest free and easy for the winter, on the snowy, lichen covered mountain tops of the Cairngorms.

SCOTTISH EXECUTIVE

Environment and Rural Affairs Department

Mr S Claus
c/o Reindeer House
Glenmore
Aviemore
Inverness-shire
PH22 1QU

Dear Sir

SPECIFIC MOVEMENT LICENCE Licence Number: RE1/ND3/3R

The Licensing team at Thainstone were deeply concerned with the reports on the media that you would be having problems getting your animals out on Christmas Eve to deliver all the toys to the girls and boys in time for Christmas Day.

We have therefore arranged for the enclosed special license to be issued on a non prejudiced basis to allow you to carryout your annual trip so that all the children can enjoy the festive season and your good name continues.

Yours sincerely

For Principal Agricultural Officer

Following the year of the Foot-and-mouth outbreak, Reindeer teams were only able to attend events in Scotland under licence. This was the final and most important permit of the season.
December 2001

In previous years, Britain has suffered outbreaks of both foot-and-mouth disease and the bluetongue virus. Reindeer, being cloven hoofed ruminants, are susceptible to both diseases and therefore are affected by the travel restrictions enforced at the time which help prevent the spread of the disease. In February 2001 an outbreak of foot-and-mouth meant that many Christmas events across Britain had to be cancelled. Movement permits were applied for and events in Scotland were permitted. Towards the end of December the Scottish and Rural Affairs Department (SERAD) sent special seasonal permission to the Reindeer Company, allowing the movement of the eight 'special' reindeer for Christmas Eve.

Training by Loch Morlich. Left to right, Bynack, Oban, Eric, and Johan pull the sleigh, which
was previously featured in an advert for a Schweppes drink.
Early 1990's
Photo: Tilly Smith

Above: Herder Sally Ward with
Christmas reindeer Grunter and Hughie
during a training session outside Reindeer
House, Glenmore.
December 2011

Right: Oasis and Shekel play with the
harness, at the end of the Christmas Day
parade, Aviemore.
25th December 2010
Photo: Tilly Smith

Christmas with reindeer Tiger and Iceberg, Crathes Castle, Banchory, 2004
Photo: Alex Smith

The reindeer Red (left) with Santa on his first outing as a Christmas reindeer. Glenmore. 2002

Fiona Smith and Magnus, 2012

Alan Smith and Wally, 1984

Alex Smith with Utsi, 2006

"READ ALL ABOUT IT"

Movies, Television & Press over the years

The BBC team with the Cairngorm herd and local children, filming on the Coire-na-Ciste road.
3rd December 1969
Photo: James Taylor

THE PRESS AND JOURNAL   FRIDAY OCTOBER 1 1976

Nethybridge reindeer centre of attraction

MEMBERS of the British Glasiological Society, who are on a Scottish field trip with Mr David Dugden, of Aberdeen University, paid a visit to Nethybridge to see Mr Mikel Utsi (holding reindeer). Mr Utsi, managing director of the British Reindeer Company, imported the reindeer into Scotland some years ago, where they are now thriving. In the foreground is a very rare albino, six-year-old Kim.

The Cairngorm Reindeer visit the local village of Nethy Bridge
1st October 1976
Press & Journal

Don't be vague. Scotch is **Haig**.

Left: Smokey, the reindeer oxen, in an advert for Haig Scotch Whisky.
20th December 1973
East Anglia Radio Times

Right: Alan Smith reading the local newspaper to Wally the reindeer in the front room of Reindeer House.
Autumn 1984

115

SEASON'S GREETINGS

Left: Christmas card from The
Royal Bank Of Scotland. The
mobile branch makes a stop
for Mikel Utsi and his reindeer,
before continuing up the ski
road to the Cairngorm Car Park
(2,083 ft).
December 1968
Photo: Royal Bank of Scotland

A skiing party are awarded the added bonus you may find in the Highlands: the sight of reindeer on the slopes.
20th October 1979
Clipping: Woman's Weekly magazine

Above: Filming an advert for Citreon cars in East London with Christmas reindeer Gustav, Mackerel, and Johan.
December 1995

Left: A Christmas promotion for Virgin trains, with Christmas reindeer Jura, catching a ride first class.
December 1996

Left: A local promotional shoot, with Santa and 'the reindeer family'. Alex, Alan, Tilly and Fiona, with reindeer Wally on the beach of Loch Morlich, Glenmore.
Winter 1987
Photo: Aviemore Photographics

Right: Desmond Morris and Sarah Kennedy with reindeer Corby and Norton, two of the eight reindeer who featured in 'Santa Claus the Movie'
Winter 1987

Left: Promoting the Christmas stamp featuring 'The Snowman' with local Postman Graham. Santa holds reindeer Black Sarek and Dubh.
Christmas 2004
Photo: Royal Mail

Right: Reindeer Crackle poses with Melanie Sykes at Covent Garden, London to promote the Christmas stamp for the Royal Mail.
December 1997
Photo: Royal Mail

Reindeer calf Fred at seven months,
featuring in the Telegraph magazine in
their Christmas centrefold.
22nd December 2001
Photos: Richard Ansett

Fiona Smith, 4, feeds Larch, one of the 100 reindeer which roam 6,000 acres of land in the Cairngorms, the only place in the UK where reindeer can be seen in the wild. The herd is looked after by Fiona's mother, Elizabeth Smith, director of the reindeer centre at Glenmore. Deer friends. Page 9

Left: Cutting from 'The Scotsman' newspaper. Fiona Smith with Larch the reindeer.
15th December 1990

Dr Oliver Dansie, Tilly's father, pays a visit to Whitwell Primary School with Wally the reindeer.
December 1993

The much loved Christmas
reindeer, Comet, poses for
the camera during the filming
for the Christmas special
of children's programme,
Ballamory.
May 2005
Photo: Tilly Smith

Above: Filming for the BBC production of 'The Lion, The Witch and The Wardrobe. Filmed during the winter of 1987 in the Glenmore Forest, close to the reindeer enclosure.

Right: Alan with the reindeer; Albert, Norton, and Cato.
Winter 1987
Photos: Tilly Smith

Filming the BBC production 'Weird Nature'. White reindeer, Milligan, helps to pull the sleigh. Filmed at the studio in Cardiff.
Photo: Tilly Smith

Eva pictured with Mr Utsi and two of the reindeer at Reindeer House.
["Herald" Photo.]

MISS WILDLIFE ENJOYED VISIT TO AVIEMORE AREA

Above: Austrian beauty queen and former Miss World, Eva von Reuber-Staier visits the Cairngorm herd on a trip to the area.
25th July 1971
Photo: Herald

Left: Bagheera and Malteser pull the sleigh for the Marks & Spencer Christmas television advert alongside the regular stars.
Filmed at Black Island Studios, London.
Sept 2006
Photo: Alex Smith

Below: Tom Baker, who played the part of 'Dr Who' between 1974 and 1981 for the BBC. He is photographed with Christmas reindeer, Donner for a promotional shoot.
1980's

ALL THE COLOURS OF THE REIN-BOW

The importance of genetics and inheriting family traits

This 2-week old reindeer calf is 'common coloured'. He has the same colourings as his wild cousin, the caribou, on the American continent. Reindeer are one of only two deer species which produce un-spotted young.
Photo: Alex Smith

Caribou and reindeer are of the same species, *Rangifer tarandus*. However, the two live on separate continents and are noticeably different in their appearances; the colour of caribou remain consistant throughout, whereas reindeer display a wide variety of colour types, due to their lengthy process of domestication. In order to achieve docile, workable herds, reindeer with favoured character attributes were selected for breeding which inadvertently resulted in the emergence of colour variations. Distinctive colour types in the reindeer became helpful for recognising bulls and family groups, therefore selective breeding for particular colours became a popular practice amongst reindeer people. With over sixty years of breeding, the herd on the Cairngorms now include many varieties of colours, though some have been encouraged more than others.

When reindeer calves are born, colours and markings are at their strongest. By the time the first winter coat has grown in, their marks are less noticeable and by their second year of a summer coat some birth markings disappear altogether.
All reindeer grow two coats in the year; the darker, thinner summer coat appears once the old winter coat has fully moulted and the transition has normally been completed by the month of July. As the season changes into the autumn, the winter coat grows in, in time for the rut in October.

The winter coat is much lighter in colour and is thicker than the summer coat. It comprises two layers; a dense woolly 'fur' layer, trapped beneath the outer guard hairs of the coat which can grow up to two inches long. Each guard hair is hollow, trapping air into the coat, providing essential insulation from subzero temperatures which are experienced throughout the snowy winter months. The reindeer are completely covered by hair from nose to tail.

The possibilities of artificial insemination were investigated by Dr Hector Dott from 1967. He was a friend of Dr Lindgren from Cambridge and he volunteered his services to the Reindeer Company for over 20 years. In that time he made several attempts to artificially inseminate some reindeer cows within the herd.

Mikel Utsi and Dr Lindgren relied upon new bulls to keep family lines free from inbreeding, therefore a number of bulls were imported from overseas. The aims of the A.I experiments were to limit the numbers of reindeer which were being imported, whilst continuing to address the gene diversity within the herd.

In 1972, two calves from the Cairngorm herd, Emma and Moulie, were believed to be the worlds' first reindeer to be born through A.I. Though the research was successful in part, it was not a realistic option for the breeding project of the reindeer on the Cairngorms.

A I PRODUCES TWO REINDEER CALVES

Two reindeer calves which have been born to two hinds of the Cairngorms herd by artificial insemination are thriving. Mr Mikel Utsi, a reindeer expert of Glenmore said this was probably the first time artificial insemination had been carried out successfully with reindeer.

The technique was being tried on the herd, founded about 20 years ago and now about 80-strong, to introduce fresh stock. "This could mean eventually that we won't need to import a bull stag from abroad," Mr Utsi said.

Kivi was bred from Russian/Finnish herds and was the father of Emma and Moulie, believed to be the first reindeer calves in the world born by Artificial Insemination.
Photo: E.J. Lindgren

Right: Dr Dott working in the enclosure with the reindeer. 1985

Emma and Moulie are doing fine

Two reindeer calves, believed to be the first in the world born by artificial insemination, are thriving in their Cairngorms herd.

Emma and Moulie are now over five months old and "doing very well," says Mr Mikel Utsi, the herdmaster, at Glenmore, Inverness-shire.

Artificial insemination is being used in an experiment on the herd—founded 20 years ago and now 80 strong—in a bid to save stag imports and cut costs.

The Courier and Advertiser, Saturday, October 28, 1972.

During his 27 years in Scotland, Mr Utsi had brought in bulls from various sources, in order to broaden the gene pool of his herd. Many reindeer were imported from Sweden and several from Norwegian reindeer herds. Large forest reindeer were also imported. A Finnish/Russian reindeer bull, Kivi, came to the herd as a gift from Whipsnade Zoo, London, and he bred for many years.

Breeding from bulls of different origins was important for effective herd management; with various gene pools spread across family lines, the herd became stronger.

Dr Lindgren continued to recognise the importance of gene diversity after her husband's death, arranging for the purchase of bulls, Rurik and Nickul, from Regents Park. Rurik descended from Russian herds and served as a bull up until 1985. After Rurik, there were no imported bulls for some time, as the herd had grown to a size where homebred bulls could be used for breeding, provided the herd could be split into breeding groups for the duration of the rut. This system worked well. By 2004, Alan and Tilly felt that it was time to 're-stock the gene pool' and bring in some reindeer from foreign herds. Rekindling connections with the Utsi family across Sweden and Norway, the couple selected reindeer from these herds to bring to Scotland.

Swedish reindeer such as Sirkas, Porjus, and Ola were imported in 2004 and became main breeding bulls for many years. Sirkas, a white faced bull, with a docile but cantankerous disposition sired a large number of white, or partially white reindeer. One of Sirkas's offspring was Blondie, a pure white reindeer, born in 2006. Her mother, Glacier, descended from a long line of 'white' reindeer, including Mikel Utsi's first white reindeer born in the herd, Snowflake, born 1968.

Paintpot is a clear example of these colourful genetic traits. His mother Shine is 'normal coloured', and his father is Sirkas. Not only does he share the striking colourful features of his father; unfortunately, he has also inherited his irritable and impatient personality!

Certificate for the importation of reindeer from Narvik, Norway to the port of Grangemouth. These were the 2nd consignment of reindeer to arrive to the herd. 24th October 1952

Top: Sirkas, the white faced Swedish bull spread the recessive white colour gene into the breeding lines in the ruts of 2004 to 2007.

Top Right: Snowflake, the first pure white reindeer born in Scotland, 1968 with her calf, Stina, born 1978.

Center: Blondie, descendent of Snowflake. She was only the second pure white reindeer of the herd, born 2006. Her female ancestors are listed to the right.

Snowflake 1968

Stina 1978

Vivi 1985

Ferrari 1991

Glacier 1996

Blondie 2006

Borneo is one of the darkest reindeer in the herd, and appeared almost jet black as a calf. He inherits his rare colouring from his Swedish father Ola, and his antlers have taken after the shape of his father's too.

Porjus and Topi are both very much alike. They share antler shape and similar colouring, although Porjus is just slightly darker than Topi, who perhaps has inherited stronger colour traits from his mother, Tuppence, who is lighter in colour. Topi and Porjus have similar markings on their foreheads, a combination of dark and white hairs giving a 'grey' appearance.

Genes carried through the female line are also often visible in the herd. A clear example of this is female Burgundy, born 1991, whose family line descended from the imported Swedish female Vilda. Burgundy, like many of her forebears, produced wonderful antlers but only managed to produce three calves in her long and healthy life. Two of her calves were male and inherited her exceptional antler genes. Burgundy and Crann's antlers are particularly similar, a clear example of the role that genes play in antler growth.

In 2009 Alan and Tilly imported reindeer from the forest variety. Forest reindeer have adapted to wading through the deep soft snow that collects beneath the trees, very different to the hard-packed snow that lies upon the exposed tundra. As a result, the forest reindeer have developed longer legs and their antlers grow closer together, enabling them to run through narrow gaps between densely grown trees of the boreal forests. Sourced from Rödingsträsk in South East Swedish Lapland, in the forests between Jokkmokk and Luleå, live a herd of reindeer which remain in the forests for the entire year. The reindeer there are renowned for their large size, and are typically tall and thickset, more so than most forest reindeer. Bajaan, Jaska and Pelle were all from Rödingsträsk and came across in 2008 with hopes that they would spread their 'super-sized' genes throughout the herd. Mikel Utsi had also sourced breeding reindeer from there in previous years.

Above: Burgundy, mother of Crann with her first calf, 'Shock'. She only produced three calves in her lifetime. Both her males grew exceptional antlers. Burgundy's antlers were very large for a female.

Right: Comparing Crann's antler with his mother, Burgundy's and his father, Cluster's. It is clear he has inherited aspects from both sides, but perhaps more from his mother.

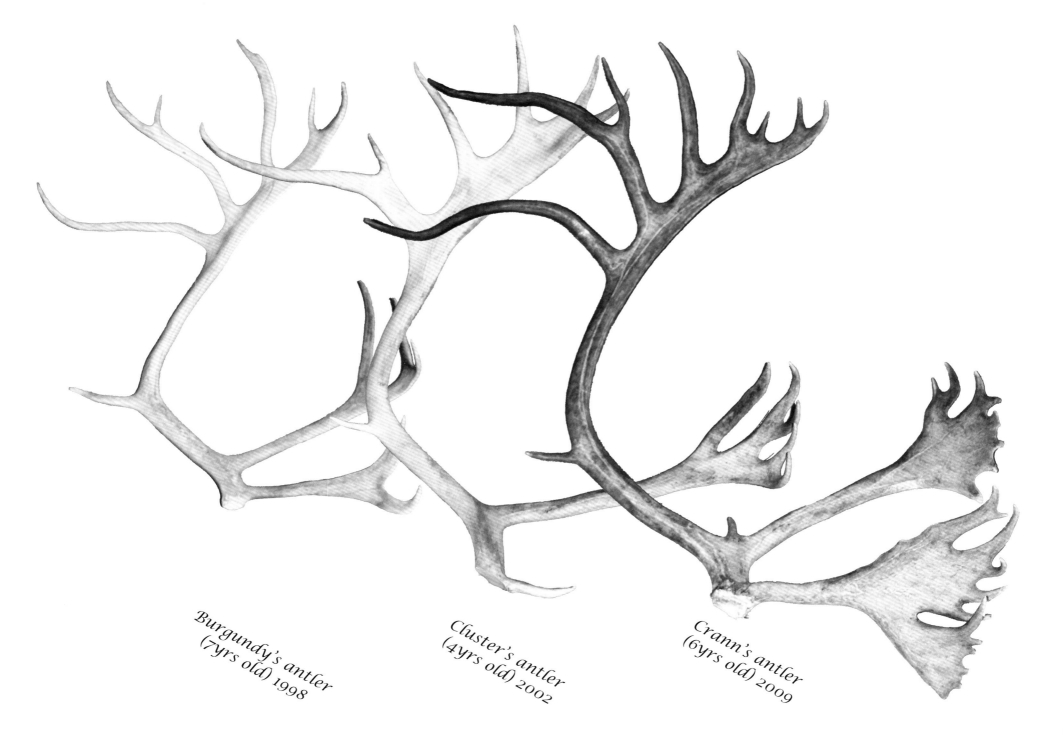

Burgundy's antler
(7yrs old) 1998

Cluster's antler
(4yrs old) 2002

Crann's antler
(6yrs old) 2009

REINDEER TAILS

Stories of reindeer from the Cairngorm Herd

the story of SAREK *the first reindeer*

In reindeer herding cultures the ox or castrated male is a very important member of the herd. As a non-breeding, or castrated male it grows strong, lives long and is docile all year round. Although today most of the Sami use motorbikes, helicopters and other motorised transport to move their reindeer and belongings around, in years gone by, the oxen would have been leaders of the herd, ridden and used as pack animals and sled pullers. In many parts of Siberia and Russia the oxen are still the main beasts of burden.

Sarek, the 2 year old Ox brought into Scotland with the first consignment of reindeer in May 1952, may have seemed to be a rather unnecessary addition to what was essentially a breeding programme. Mr Utsi was hoping to do more than reintroduce reindeer back into Scotland, he was also bringing part of his Sami culture with him. Indeed in the 1950's, the castrated males still played an important role in Sami life, as part of a team of oxen who were regularly handled, harnessed and acted as the 'tame' connection to the rest of the herd, the wilder bulls, cows and calves.

Named by Mr Utsi after a mountain range in Swedish Lapland and the ship on which he travelled to Scotland, Sarek provided stability to the small group of imported reindeer, and with a bell around his neck he was the herd leader. Mr Utsi always made mention of Sarek as if he were his friend and companion. Numerous photos were taken of the two of them together in the Cairngorms and Sarek went on to lead the herd for many years. He went missing at the grand old age of 16 years, and was assumed to have died quietly and peacefully, within the Cairngorm mountains.

" *Sarek, nearly sixteen,
had been missing for some weeks, Mr Utsi said that in
August the old leader had come back after weeks of solitude
somewhere; but now "perhaps he has
gone to rest".* "

Extract from The Directors Meetings of
the Reindeer Co. Ltd.
16th January 1965

the story of # KIVI *the Russian reindeer*

Born: May 1971   Died: 24th December 1977

The herd was growing well by the late 60's and early 70's. Whipsnade Zoological Park had called to inform Mr Utsi that they had a bull of Finnish and Russian lineage that they wished to part with.

He arrived into the herd on the 25th September 1972 as a yearling. He was capable of breeding but was by no means fully grown.

Over the years, Kivi grew into a fine bull and outgrew all the reindeer in the herd. Russian reindeer tend to be larger than their Scandinavian cousins and so Kivi was an important asset to the herd.

During the stalking season of September 1972, Mr Utsi feared that his prime breeding bull would be mistaken for a Red deer stag, as many were still unaware of the existence of reindeer in the Cairngorms. To ease his worry, he tied a red flag to Kivi's grand antlers as an obvious alert to hunters that he was not for the table.

Kivi reached a good age for such a large and prolific breeding male, dying at the age of 8 on the 24th of December 1977.

He was the first animal to be used for the research of artificial insemination in reindeer; the first two reindeer to be concieved by this method were born in 1972. During his lifetime, Kivi fathered a large number of calves, many of which became successful breeders themselves. Today, the Scottish-bred herd of reindeer still have a little (or large) amount of the Russian Kivi left in them!

Kivi, as a young bull, photographed within the 'East Enclosure' 10 days after his arrival to join the herd.
He grew extremely impressive antlers, unusual for a yearling.
1st Oct 1972

the story of BOKO *the handreared reindeer*

Born: 8th May 1962   Died: 14th December 1967
Mother: Laila   Father: Vikhta

Mr Utsi hand reared a reindeer calf in 1962 when Laila, an imported cow from Norway, died 12 hours after she had calved. Her bull calf was dark in colour and a good weight at 12 lbs. He was feisty, keen and quickly took to a milk substitute, fed from a bottle. Mr Utsi named him Boko. The two were rarely apart for long spells. Mr Utsi was very protective of Boko and he cared for him like a child.

Mr Utsi spent much of his time at their home in Harston, Cambridge. The 500 mile journey from Reindeer House was a slow and arduous drive so Mr Utsi would normally stop halfway at a guesthouse or hotel en route. While Boko was just a calf he accompanied Mr Utsi on one of his trips South. Needing a rest to break the journey, Mr Utsi wandered into a hotel, with Boko following close at his heels. On seeing Mr Utsi's companion the horrified receptionist shrieked that "goats are not allowed!". Mr Utsi was so furious that his beloved Boko was referred to as a goat and was not allowed to stay that he promptly left and vowed never to return to that particular hotel again.

Mr Utsi took Boko with him everywhere he went. He appeared both in and out of doors at the cities of Inverness, Edinburgh, Cambridge, Wethersfield and even visited the Metropolitan Police Cadet Corps Training School in Hendon. He won many new friends for the Glenmore herd, and was often featured in local newspaper articles. He was often seen 'out and about' in Glenmore. At the campsite he and Mr Utsi would visit friends in their caravans, or take walks down to the loch side. During one particularly hot summer, after a run of warm, sunny days, Mr Utsi took Boko along with his draught ox Nikka for a swim in nearby Loch Morlich, to the amazement of the many tourists who had probably never seen a reindeer before, let alone seen a strange looking man swimming happily alongside two of them!

Boko grew into a particularly bold reindeer and, being so tame and fearless, he became troublesome in the rut. There are numerous accounts of him hounding skiers and walkers out on the Cairngorms but, upon receiving these complaints of his behaviour, Mr Utsi would always loyally defend Boko. He was his favourite breeding bull, having descended from Norwegian lines and been lovingly raised by him.

In 1966, when Boko was 4 years old, it was suggested that Boko be "reduced to the ranks of gelding" by other members of the Reindeer Company. Despite objections by Mr Utsi, Boko was finally gelded in November 1966. In May '67, just 6 months afterwards, Mr Utsi was informed of a complaint placed in mid-March that "a reindeer had pawed and nuzzled a skier who had fallen on the nursery slopes", the same reindeer having foraged "amongst rucksacks and bags belonging to skiers". It had become apparent that, despite being gelded, Boko was still misbehaving and simply could not be trusted.

Rather than leave him unsupervised on the mountains, Mr Utsi took Boko once again with him to Cambridge on the 22nd October 1967. Whilst there a foot-and-mouth outbreak put Britain on a standstill and Boko became stranded; the return journey was made impossible due to the movement restrictions that applied to all cloven hoofed animals. Reindeer can tolerate the milder climates of the South of England temporarily, but longer periods spent there can expose them to fatal diseases. So it was that on the 14th December Boko suddenly sickened. His fever rose to 41.7 C (his normal body temperature being 38.9 C) and just an hour after having been treated by a vet, Boko died.

After his death, Dr Lindgren wrote that Boko was "*an outstandingly handsome, vital, uncannily intelligent and wayward animal. Expressions of sympathy for Mr Utsi personally and for the company in their loss were expressed by a large number of people in Britain and abroad. Surviving through his progeny in the herd and recorded by photographs, drawings and descriptions in the press, Boko was assured of a permanent place in the history of reindeer breeding, not only in Scotland.*"

Vincent Utsi and Keith Simpson with Boko, only 2 months old. Boko slept outside "like a guard dog" while they camped below Coire na Sneachda in the Cairngorms.
28th July 1962
Photo: M Buchanan

the story of **NADIA** *the breeding female*

Born: 19th May 1973 *Died: Winter 1987/88*
Mother: Nan *Father: Kivi*

Nadia was born on 19th May 1973 to Nancy. Known as Nan, Nancy was born in Scotland on 14th May 1962 to Vilda, one of the original imported reindeer.

Nadia's father was the large Russian reindeer, Kivi. She was among his first offspring and named according to the theme of the year (1973) 'Russian names'. She was mis-sexed at birth, thought to be a male and was named Ivan. When it was realised that she was in fact female, she was given the more suitable and pretty name of Nadia. She was common-coloured and exceptionally tame, even as a calf.

By the time she had matured into a breeding female it was clear she had inherited many of her attributes from Kivi, as she was larger than all of the other females in the herd. She grew splendid antlers and throughout her life continued to be mistaken for a bull by those who did not know her.

She was a natural leader in the herd and the reindeer followed her loyally. She was easy to catch and to halter and was favoured as a 'lead reindeer' by herder, Alan.

By 1982, she was so large and docile that she shared the work of the male 'Christmas reindeer', posing alongside Santa on Christmas events. Being so good looking, she took to the spotlight and featured in a Christmas promotional magazine for Selfridges, London.

Nadia's most successful female calf was her first born in 1977, named Natasha. She was a strong reindeer from birth but did not grow to be as large or impressive as her mother. As if to compensate, she went on to become the most prolific breeder in the entire herd. Over her long life of 14 years, she managed to produce 13 calves in total - certainly a record in the Cairngorm herd, easily making her one of the most successful female reindeer in the world!

Extracted from the Director's Reports, 1983. Written by Dr Lindgren.

" *What the public will see in 1983 Christmas magazines is a colourful full page advertisement showing Nadia harnessed to a fairy tale type sleigh over flowing with parcels, standing placidly on 'snow' in the middle of Oxford Street with the spectacular illuminations of a famous store in the background. Dr Lindgren, who was part of the team on this occasion, had been promised that all traffic would be stopped from 1 am to 4 am on 14th December and that a representative of the animal hiring firm, for which the Reindeer Company had once before fulfilled an engagement, would be present throughout. Neither promise was fulfilled. Traffic flowed almost continuously in spite of the early hour and, although police cars were parked on both sides of the scene, there was only a few seconds' pause when the photographer was seen to be pressing the button. The temperamental crew employed by the advertisers dithered and dallied over details while the whole landscape was gradually sprayed with artificial snow. The slight young lady sent by the animal suppliers was soon frozen through on that exceptionally bitter night and excused herself at 1 am The Aviemore horse-box driver, already exhausted and with the long journey back before him, retired to bed three hours later at the nearby hotel.*

Dr Lindgren's task was to exercise and feed lichen to the reindeer, Keith, on the pavement, which went fairly smoothly despite Keith's restlessness until Nadia, menaced and almost grazed by noisy buses and cars, refused to stand quietly any longer or look in the right direction unless Keith was precisely in her line of sight.

After 5 am twelve pictures were finally taken, at a leisurely pace, with Alan Smith each time squatting on his heels in front of Nadia, face to face but out of view of the camera. Just before the last photograph was taken Keith suddenly became hysterical and, despite his youth, managed to fling a substantial male bystander who was trying to help restrain him into the air. As the victim descended, Dr Lindgren quenched his indignation by making him a present of Keith's remaining antler, which had broken off in the stranger's hand.

"Wonderful shot!" muttered the chief of the advertisers in passing, as the whole party scattered. Alan Smith led both reindeer back to the horse box, parked in a bay within Selfridge's complex, and stopped the bleeding at the base of Keith's antler with a 'wonder salve', always carried in Dr Lindgren's suitcase. At 6:30 a.m the hotel porter said a courteous 'good night' to the Keeper and Secretary, both frozen to the marrow, as they finished their last cup of coffee in the front hall.

Selfridges
Autumn/Winter 1983 MAGAZINE

the story of # COMET *the beloved Christmas reindeer*

Born: 1st May 1995   Died: 5th April 2012
Mother: Ferrari   Father: Crackle

Comet's mother Ferrari was born in Scotland in 1991 and was an extremely prolific breeder. From the age of 2, she calved every year, alternating the sex of her calf each time. She took a break from calving in the year 2001, but continued thereafter until she had surpassed reindeer life expectancy, still managing to calve at the grand old age of 14. She finally died just before her 17th birthday, making her one of the longest living reindeer throughout the herd's history. She was a descendent of Assa, who was brought to Scotland by Mr Utsi from Sweden in 1952.

Within Assa's large family are many white reindeer, including Ferrari. White reindeer are considered special in many reindeer cultures across the world. They hold a place of spiritual importance and, as such, are revered by reindeer herders. Because of reindeer like Comet, it is easy to understand why.

Comet was born on the 1st May 1995 and was Ferrari's third calf. He was the tamest reindeer of his year and he grew up into a fine looking bull, with large antlers and a gentle personality. At the age of 2, he was used as a breeding bull for just one year. He fathered other tame Christmas reindeer, such as Utsi, Minstrel and Trebor, all of whom adopted Comet's laid back and tame disposition. Comet was gelded at the age of 3 and trained to become a 'Christmas reindeer'. As his name would suggest, he learnt to pull the sleigh effortlessly, taking to it like a duck to water. He always had a very calming effect on the other reindeer he worked with, and even in his younger years he behaved with an air of wisdom and grace. He was loved by all who met him because of his gentle nature. Young children on the Hill Visit could clamber over him, stroking and hugging him, while Comet just stood there, patiently and proudly.

He gained much support for the herd over his many years, acquiring a record number of adopters, who would repeatedly travel up to see him, visiting him like an old friend.

He worked through many Christmas seasons, but as he grew older, Santa became too heavy for him and the amount of travelling grew tiring. Comet was therefore given the relief work of helping to train the younger and more impatient reindeer back with the herd at home. His calming presence would often be enough to reassure the most nervous trainee; in no time at all Comet would work his magic and another Christmas reindeer would be fully trained and bomb-proof!

He would visit the local schools, always receiving the same reaction; everyone who met him would fall in love with him. He was always an extremely popular reindeer, to both children and adults alike.

Children would often confide in Comet with their Christmas wishes, whispering into his ear. They would lie down next to him, alone on the open hillside and he would never get up.

Reindeer are not loud animals and they don't make many noises, but some are more restless than others. The aura around Comet was always peaceful and silent.

Comet eventually died at the grand old age of 16, a month away from his 17th birthday, living to the same age as his mother. He passed away in his sleep far away on the mountainside. It was a gentle way to go, but then there was no gentler reindeer than Comet.

the story of ARNISH *the bold, but antlerless reindeer*

Born: 2nd May 1997   Died: Winter 2011/12
Mother: Tarn   Father: Plum

Within the deer family, there are approximately 40 separate species and reindeer are just one of them. Reindeer are exceptional; they are the only arctic species of deer and they are also the only species in which every single deer has the ability to grow antlers, whether they are a female (cow), a newly born calf, a reindeer ox (gelded male) or, of course, a breeding male (bull). A sure way to climb up the ranks for dominance, antlers are extremely beneficial. They can be used to compete for food, as a defence against predators, as a display of strength, and for competing with bulls to fight for the right to breed during the rut. It is safe to say that antlers come in very handy.

Both females and males have a turn at the top. All antlers are grown over the Spring, when grazing is at it's richest and then the antlers are stripped of the velvet (the hairy layer of skin which carries blood vessels while the antler is growing). The reindeer are left with hard, bony antlers by the beginning of Autumn. The breeding males are most dominant during the rut, but they keep their antlers for the shortest time; dropping them before the end of the year. Here, the females take position at the top of the herd and with their antlers are able to push the large, hungry males away while they spend precious energy digging and foraging for lichens growing deep under the snow. The calves and oxen also find it useful to have antlers when competing for food; the bigger the headwear, the better!

Arnish's mother, Tarn, grew a fine set of antlers. Her father Plum's antlers were particularly large, but Arnish never sprouted a single bump. Antlers can vary in size and quality from year to year depending on the condition of the individual, and for some reindeer it's just a matter of time but by the time Arnish had reached full maturity with still no sign of growing any, it was accepted that Arnish was to be an antler-less reindeer and would no doubt be at the bottom of the pecking order her whole life.

This was not so. As Arnish grew older she became one of the boldest, bravest and bossiest reindeer of all. The other females went to so much trouble year after year, putting all of their energy into growing the biggest antlers, while Arnish used all of her energy into simply *being* the biggest!

She was always seen leading the herds out on the mountains, acting as matriarch, she would make decisions for the herd on where they should go to graze and which routes they should take. The rest of the herd would follow her loyally, comfortable that Arnish was in charge.

When two separate and unfamiliar herds meet, it is necessary for each individual to re-assert its dominance so that each reindeer's 'rank' can be ascertained. On one such event, the herds from the free-range had been gathered into the enclosure, in preparation for the rutting season. Arnish and her 'followers' were first in. The following group arrived a little later and were led by an extremely dominant female, Shine. Shine had great antlers, with long, forward pointing tines. She was a very strong female and would certainly be a challenge to beat. Arnish walked up to her with her head down. She gave Shine one sidelong stare before charging towards her at full speed. Spectators winced as her eyes, unprotected by any antler of her own, moved close to Shine's, but with sheer determination and summoning such strength, Arnish powered forward, causing Shine to lose her footing and as if to clarify her status further, reared up onto her hind legs and thumped Shine with her front hooves in a slapping motion. Shine accepted defeat and shrunk away, choosing to graze at a greater distance from Arnish. Arnish promptly moved on to challenge every other female who thought a little too highly of themselves and their antlers, in order to keep up her reputation as 'Arnish, the rather awesome yet antler-less reindeer cow'!

the story of **CRANN** *the Scottish reindeer bull*

Born 21st May 2003
Mother: Burgundy   Father: Cluster

Out of all the species within the deer family, it is the reindeer which grow the largest antlers in relation to their body size. The Scottish-born bull, Crann, certainly supports this fact. Large antlers from both his mother, Burgundy's side and his father, Crackle's, were passed on to Crann, who from a young age, grew antlers that outsized all the other reindeer of his year. By the time Crann had reached full maturity at five years old, his antlers weighed 8kg. The following few years he grew even larger sets and the weight of his antlers in his eighth year had reached a whopping 10kg. Undoubtably, Crann has grown the largest antlers of any reindeer throughout the entire history of the herd. His grew even larger than his Russian predecessor Kivi.

Crann's antler tactics are perhaps in his timings. He was always extremely early in growing his new set of antlers; typically it is in March when the reindeer bulls can be seen sprouting the beginnings of new antlers, but Crann begins as early as January! He also has the largest appetite of all the reindeer and is lazy too, allowing priority to his antler growth over everything else. When not eating he lies around, careful not to waste any energy. By the time he has finished growing his antlers, he then concentrates his energies on his body size, arriving into the rut a little rounded at the edges.

Unfortunately for Crann, his attitude and strength in the rut did not match his superior antlers. When facing Swedish bull Mosski in a fight over the harem females, he was eventually outmanoeuvred. It was a close fight and a long one, lasting over 20 minutes, eventually Mosski won with the advantage of both stamina and fitness, despite having grown a far less impressive set of antlers

© Les Wilson

and proving that appearances can be deceiving. Crann could be described as a vain reindeer, he concentrates all his energy on his fancy looks, when perhaps he would be wiser to devote more of his energy in 'keeping fit'.

Having such long, sweeping antlers he was given an extremely wide berth by reindeer herders during the rut, but, once the rut had passed Crann returned to his usual laid back, 'soft as putty' self and he kept his antlers on for as long as he was able until the day finally arrived when they both fell off.

When Crann loses his antlers, it can become a bit of a drama. On one occasion he lost one of his antlers about a week prior to losing the other. With such a heavy weight being lifted from just one side of his head, it meant an awful lot of compensation was needed to keep his head straight - consequently through this time he was noted to be walking sideways an awful lot!

All reindeer eventually lose their antlers; the bulls drop them usually during November, the oxen keep them ideally through to the next year, and the females keep them the longest, through the winter and up to calving in May. However, there are no exact timings, so witnessing this event is all down to chance. Whilst Crann was staying for a short time in the Paddocks to the back of Reindeer House in November, Tilly was lucky enough to witness one evening as Crann's antlers dropped from his head to the floor. You would think that to suddenly lose 10kg of weight bearing down on your head would bring a feeling of relief, however, on this occassion Crann looked grief ridden - he looked down at his beautiful antlers lying on the floor and was visibly shaking. To lose such large antlers instantly meant losing all of his superiority within the herd. But, fortunately for Crann, and indeed for all of the herd, the reindeer are given another chance to be 'at the top' again with the arrival of Spring, when they can begin growing a brand new set, even bigger and better than before. Crann's antlers are invariably something to look forward to.

the story of LILAC *the wild reindeer*

Born: 7th May 1999
Mother: Sundew   Father: Etienne

Lilac was born on 7th May 1999 to Sundew who descended from imported Swedish reindeer Assa, brought into Scotland by Mikel Utsi in 1952.

Lilac is a strong and capable reindeer, is extremely independent and certainly has a mind of her own. She is exceptionally greedy and will follow the herder eagerly (if bribed by food). Unfortunately, as soon as she becomes suspicious of the herder's motives she will double back in an instant. She seems to do this once the herder, after much time, has managed to move the reindeer across miles of rough mountain terrain. As if to mock the herder's painstaking efforts, Lilac will then run at full speed in the opposite direction, leaving behind an exhausted and frustrated herder, who can only attempt in vain to stop the rest of the herd following in her speedy foot-steps.

On one occasion, on account of her usual, disruptive behaviour ,she was caught and haltered and led at the front, whilst the other reindeer followed behind. Lilac did not at this moment wish to be 'led' and so mustering all her strength she pulled the rope out from the herders hand, and ran off up the mountain wearing her halter and trailing her rope behind. After an exhausting few hours of searching, she was finally found and released from her halter.

At the end of 2002 Lilac and a group of young female reindeer were moved across to join the herd on the Cromdale hills at Glenlivet. Here they all settled in well, except for Lilac. Soon after her

arrival, she promptly vanished. Unfamiliar to the area, it was feared she had become lost. The Cromdales were searched high and low, but to no avail. Quite remarkably, Lilac appeared three weeks later none the worse for wear at the 11 O'clock Hill Visit on the Cairngorms along with the rest of the herd - over 30 miles away!

Evidently she had managed to navigate across roads, rivers and fences to find her way home. Needless to say, she was not moved back to Glenlivet (she had made her point) Lilac now stays firmly on the Cairngorms.

Lilac has been a very successful breeder and has managed to produce 9 calves over her 13 years. Her male calves have all been calm and tame, growing into much loved 'Christmas reindeer'. Her only 2 female offspring, perhaps having spent more time with Lilac, have become just as wild, if not wilder than their mother. Both have grown into strong and independent reindeer but both are resolutely unreliable in a herding situation.

Despite her rebellious behaviour, Lilac is a wonderful reindeer. She is extremely spirited and very capable, and without a doubt must have the greatest navigational skills of all the reindeer in Scotland!

the story of MAGNUS *the tame reindeer*

Born: May 2007
Mother and Father: Swedish, unknown

From time to time new breeding bulls are sourced from outside the Cairngorm herd to bring fresh genetics into the blood lines. In the year of 2008 Sofia Baer and her sister Miliana, great nieces of Mikel Utsi, sourced a small group of reindeer from their family's herd in the north of Sweden. Magnus was among them. Fiona spent time with them familiarising them with people and being handled before they arrived to Scotland. Some reindeer never become tame, others require a lot of work before they get there, but a few seemingly are tame from birth. Magnus is of the latter kind.

He is the epitome of domestication in reindeer. This process of domestication of reindeer has led to a multitude of coat colours among the Scandinavian and Russian herds. Reindeer owners are able to identify animals easily from a distance by their distinctive markings. For this reason, over hundreds of years, reindeer have been selectively bred for their colours, markings and temperament. With his patchy, white face, Magnus's looks are very distinctive and being extremely friendly, his character is distinctive also. When he was selected from hundreds of other reindeer, Sofia wrote to Reindeer House, "*You're going to love this one*". She could see right from the start that there was something special about Magnus, aside from his distinctive markings, because, despite having never been around people before, he was already tame.

Whilst in quarantine in Sweden, before journeying to Scotland, Magnus fell very ill and weak and the only way to keep him from catching a chill in the Arctic winter was to move him into a sheltered spot out of the harsh elements, so Fiona moved him into Miliana's sauna. After 3 days Magnus had cheered up, he was bright and well again and was able to rejoin the others. They all arrived safely in Scotland later that year.

Being brought 'back from the brink' has perhaps encouraged Magnus's apparent attachment to humans. After their arrival to Scotland his fellow Swedes maintained their 'wild' side for quite some time, whilst Magnus behaved more like a dog, preferring to follow the herders, rather than the herd. During Hill Visits, he follows the visitors and unlike other reindeer, who enjoy their personal space, he takes delight in being stroked and fussed.

He has a habit of surprising visitors by appearing right next to them. When they turn around they are shocked to see that such a large and striking creature has managed to sneak by them, unnoticed. Another special Magnus feature is that he is the only reindeer that can be seen 'smiling'; if you look at photos of him, you'll notice his mouth is much more up-turned than any other reindeer! It is undisputed by every reindeer herder in Scotland that Magnus is the tamest and friendliest reindeer that they have had the pleasure of knowing.

In 2011, along with a group of males, Magnus was moved onto the Cromdale hills at Glenlivet. The herd there were checked regularly and Magnus would casually wander up to the herder, often without the others. After a couple of weeks, Magnus disappeared. Searches were made but he was not found anywhere. It seemed so out of character for Magnus not to walk up to meet the herder. Weeks later, to everyone's relief, tracks were spotted further down the mountain, on a path not far from Alan and Tilly's farm- but Magnus was not found. Yet another week passed, with no more signs, until a local rang to report that Magnus was in his shed! The neighbour, upon hearing a disturbance outside of his house had peered outside his back door, but had seen only tracks in the snow. Returning to the living room, he and his wife had been surprised to see Magnus's friendly face peering in at them through the window. They alerted Tilly and Alan, who arrived with a trailer minutes after receiving the call and Magnus calmly and contentedly walked up the ramp into the trailer - it was time to go home. He was in fine condition when he was found and still no-one knows exactly where he had got to on his walkabout. Perhaps he was searching for a sauna!

REINDEER REFLECTIONS

looking back on sixty years

In the past, other attempts have been made to re-introduce reindeer to Scotland, but none of them were successful. So why did Mikel Utsi and his wife Dr Lindgren triumph, where others had failed? Without a doubt, it was due to the combined efforts of them both. Dr Lindgren, with her intellect, her skills in diplomacy, and her contacts in 'high places', held the reins of the project throughout its inauguration. While Mikel Utsi's charm, his positivity and drive, and crucially, his expert knowledge and understanding of reindeer gave the project credibility from the start.

Through his Sami upbringing in Northern Sweden, Mikel Utsi knew that reindeer benefited enormously from their freedom. He understood their habits of seasonal migration, their domestic, yet wild nature and fundamentally, the importance of natural grazing. After recognising the abundance of lichens and other Arctic vegetation, seeing the vastness of the high plateaux and experiencing the Arctic environment of the high tops, he knew that reindeer belonged on the Cairngorm Mountains of Scotland. In the moment that he selected the Cairngorms as a home for the reindeer, he assured their future in Scotland.

Mr Utsi and Dr Lindgren were devoted to the reindeer and the project and together they formed a formidable team. They established the Reindeer Company and set the foundations for the herd. Originally, the objectives for the 'reindeer breeding project' were to provide a meat source and to investigate the possibilities for grazing reindeer in areas where sheep and cattle failed to thrive. Reindeer meat was sold in the UK up until the late '70's but there was never as high a demand for it as it was thought there would be. As the extraordinary couple became more widely known across Britain, the popularity of the herd spread. People wanted to see the famous reindeer, in their natural home, alongside their rare and remarkable owner, Mr Utsi. The unexpected enthusiasm from the public encouraged their move to promote revenue through tourism. From early on, the reindeer became a 'display herd' and attracted a vast number of people to the area.

When Mr Utsi died, he left his wife in charge. She came to depend on the main herder at the time, Alan Smith. He had arrived at the age of 18 and had learnt quickly, excelling in almost all of his tasks. She admired him for his natural ability and affinity with the reindeer. He was capable and cared a great deal for the welfare of the herd, devoting much of his time to the search of strays when members of the herd wandered too far. However, he lacked the administrative skills required for the job. When Elizabeth Dansie arrived, as an academic and enthusiastic post graduate zoologist, it was clear from the start that the two worked well together and, just like Mr Utsi and Dr Lindgren before them, they complemented each other perfectly. It was a natural transition for Alan and Tilly to take the reins of the Company in 1989 after the death of Dr Lindgren. They continue to this day to work with the reindeer and are as devoted to the herd as they are to each other. The reindeer have been to them, an extended family. The 'job' has become a way of life.

The ancestral roots of many of the Scottish reindeer lie in the North of Sweden and in Mikel Utsi's original herd. This herd has since been inherited by members of the Utsi family, many of whom still live by reindeer today. Alan and Tilly have maintained a close connection with the Utsi family and continue to embrace Sami culture as a cornerstone in the history of the Scottish herd.

Alan and Tilly continue to handle and manage the reindeer in a traditional way, as they were once taught, but they have developed the Reindeer Company through experimental and untraditional ideas. From these ideas, the Reindeer Company has successfully grown into a thriving business. The Reindeer Centre, the Adoption Scheme, the Hill Visits scheduled throughout the year, the Reindeer Trekking and the expansion of Christmas events have all diversified the traditional uses of reindeer and the original purposes of the herd- food and clothing. All the income gained from these ventures is circulated back into the reindeer, to further ensure their welfare.

Today, the Reindeer Centre is run by a highly competent team of staff. Each member has expert knowledge of reindeer and a keen understanding of their heritage and life in Scotland. Both of Alan and Tilly's children, Alex and Fiona, have grown up to become increasingly involved with the management of the reindeer over recent years. Their entire life has been centred around the reindeer and undoubtedly it will continue to be that way for years to come. They are Britain's first generation of native reindeer herders.

For the last sixty years reindeer have lived on the Cairngorms, in their natural environment. They have made these mountains their home and can be found there living alongside other Arctic animals such as the snow bunting, the mountain hare and the ptarmigan. They all fit together perfectly, in Britain's last surviving Arctic habitat.

The reindeer are subtle, quiet, inconspicuous animals and in such a vast area, they can easily go by unnoticed.

So, when walking in the Cairngorms, be careful to keep an eye open for hoof prints, for they've been there for a very long time.